MW00882928

Advanced Reading, Writing, and Grammar

For Test Prep

LIKE TEST PREP

DEDICATION

To LIKE Family

CONTENTS

Advanced Reading, Writing, and Grammar

How to Prepare for
Reading & Writing Tests-1

1. Learn to build your own perspective: You need to have your unique perspective about the world. That is the first step. Then, you should also practice shifting perspectives and comparing and contrasting two or more ideas. For example, think how you would strengthen or weaken the author's argument. What kind of evidence would you use to further support his/her argument? What would you do to make the author's argument sound weak? Going through such practice, you can read and write more critically. Never underestimate the reading passages or writing topics, as they derive from the acclaimed works of well-educated authors. Moreover, these authors rarely present black and white arguments. This is often done to persuade more readers. By partially accepting their opponents claim, the author prevents himself/herself from being refuted by the readers. Remember, writing is also a form of communication between readers and writers.

How to Prepare for
Reading & Writing Tests -2

2. Know what you are about to read beforehand: Any standardized reading test like the SAT or GRE contains at least one science, one socio-political, and one literary or art passage. All these passages are based on philosophy called, "multiple perspectives." In other words, one can always see things from many different perspectives. Science usually deals with physics as it is the most conceptual and philosophical. Sometimes paleontology, plate-tectonics or biology is covered. When the passage discusses biology, it is usually about taxonomy or how to classify animals and plants. When the passage discusses the environment or nature, it is usually about how to deal with pollution or treat the endangered species more effectively. Also learn the following science terms. Observation, Interpretation, Correlation, Causality (Cause and Effect), Hypothesis, Claim, Validity, Reliability. Methodology. Are you familiar with them? If not, you'd better start your research now.

How to Prepare for
Reading & Writing Tests -3, 4, 5

3. **Fill up the word/page limit**: Hundreds of thousands of students take tests like the SAT worldwide. Many actually fill up both pages to fully develop their ideas and provide many good examples. Writing 2 pages in 25 minutes is an art. For computerized writing tests like the GRE, write a lot. Many writing researches reveal that excellent essays are long. It takes time and space to fully explain one's idea. Quantity does matter.

4. **Use historical or literary examples**: Avoid using hypothetical examples or personal examples. Historical examples are persuasive because they are mostly facts and are well-accepted by the majority of people in the society. However, personal examples or rare occasions can be more easily refuted because they are not as universally known or accepted. Your readers can argue back saying, "So, what?"

5. **Use difficult words appropriately**: It is a real challenge to use the newly learned SAT/GRE vocabulary in one's own writing. That is why you need to read more and practice using them now. This way, your word usage will come more naturally.

How to Prepare for
Reading & Writing Tests -6

6. Read history, classic science and literature: It is very important that you learn new vocabulary in a context. One way to do so is by reading history. Are any of the following words familiar to you? suffragist, misogyny, affirmative action, segregation policy, Bohemian, transcendentalism, martial law, abolitionist. How about the following authors? Charles Dickens, Jane Austin, Dostoyevsky, Rousseau, Voltaire, Descartes, and Mark Twain? By reading history and classics, you can familiarize yourself with old styled writings which frequently appear in SAT reading and writing.

How to Prepare for
Reading & Writing Tests -7

7. Read the most current literature and political/social issues: Many reading passages and writing topics come from fairly recent political, scientific, and literary writers. Have you read Howard Gardener(Psychologist) or Jumpa Lahiri (novelist)? Good readers and writers also read the most acclaimed recent publications. You can easily search these authors and their titles by typing Nobel or Pulitzer winners, writers or authors. For socio-political, and science authors, Google 100 most influential professors in the world. The list will also give you the names of the finest scholars currently working in their fields.

READING
1. SENTENCE COMPLETION QUESTIONS 1

If you are a poor reader trying to beat the SAT/GRE, the first step for you is to master the sentence completion questions and short passages. Why? Because both easy and difficult questions are worth the same point. Why not harvest more scores by focusing on the easy questions first?

Before we start, please be aware that all sentence completion sentences are grammatically correct. In other words, it is the meaning that counts.

Also, study a lot of commonly appearing vocabulary, synonyms, word roots (stems), prefixes and suffixes. These, too, can boost your scores immediately.

Since I don't know where you are with SAT pr GRE vocabulary, I would like you to do a set of sentence completion questions. Give yourself 5-10 min. to finish the test and score it. Once you are done, I will explain to you my approach to this particular section.

Sentence Completion Questions Set 1

1. Jane often _____ her school work, waiting till the very last moment.

(A) delves (B) expedites (C) assumes (D) procrastinates
(E) conducts

2. The newspaper reporter had a reputation for her fair evaluation, but he was recently criticized for writing a _____ article by her critics.

(A) biased (B) dubious (C) disinterested (D) provocative
(E) equitable

3. _____ for his hideous crimes, the _____ arguably deserved capital punishment.

(A) Recognized..minor
(B) Famous..superstar
(C) Oblivious..malefactor
(D) Disreputable..victim
(E) Notorious..felon

4. Even more financially _____ than his latest bestsellers is his debut book: Rich Dad and Poor Dad.

(A) profound (B) sound (C) naive (D) ineffectual
(E) unproductive

5. Since one of the design for the upcoming fashion show was stolen, the designer had to go through all of his past works to gather ideas for a new _____.

(A) nicety (B) stipulation (C) paragon (D) bargain (E) prototype

6. The doctor approved of Myra's leave only after giving her nurse _____ instructions on the patient's medication, physical therapy, and check-ups.

(A) banal (B) redundant (C)specific (D) limited
(E) magnanimous

7. The advertising campaign for the new theme park was a _____; it was costly, mistargeted, and unappealing

(A) blunder (B)fiasco (C) success (D) affliction (E) boon

8. It was obvious that the newly recruited soccer player would increase the team morale; he was truly more than a _____.

(A) transaction (B) loss   (C) solution   (D) envoy (E) surrogate

9. The judges at the speech contest was amazed to see such touching speech delivered by a _____.

(A)fledgling (B) guru (C) connoisseur (D) veteran (E) pundit

Before I explain to you about my approaches, let's talk about your scores. There were 18 questions total and if your score was below 70 percent or less than 12, I suggest you spend more time on vocabulary and the sentence completion section alone.

Definition Types

The first type you are going to face is definition type. This type usually gives you the clues through a definition. In other words, you would have to figure out what the word for the blank is by looking at the other parts.

1. Jane often _____ her school work, waiting till the very last moment.

(A) delves (B) expedites (C) assumes (D) procrastinates
(E) conducts

In this question, the answer is D because "waiting till the last moment" is the key. It basically provides the readers with the definition of the word that would go into the blank, which means to "delay."

Contrastive Signals & Negative Words

Negative words hint you the contrastive meaning or sentence structure. Here is a list of negative words you should watch out for.

but, however, yet, despite, in contrast, rather than, on the other hand, still, although, even though, nevertheless, less, no matter, not, no, non-(prefix), anti-, in-, il-, im-(prefix), -less(suffix),

Remember that every time one of these words appear, the meaning changes to the opposite. So, watch out for them carefully as some of these could be almost hidden.

2. The newspaper reporter had a reputation for her fair evaluation, but he was recently criticized by her critics for writing a _____ article.

(A) biased (B) dubious (C) disinterested (D) provocative (E) equitable

Words like "disinterested" or "provocative" are tempting. Since the newspaper reporter has a good reputation, we might simply assume that the word that goes into the blank should be "even-handed" or "well-written." However, in this question, we need to look for the opposite word for "fair," and that is "biased." So, the answer is A.

Causality (Cause & Effect/Reason) Signals

Here is a list of words that represent causality. In other words, one cause the other to happen.

> therefore, thus, so, ultimately, consequently, because, in order to, through, since, for, incur, cause, ensue, entail, accordingly, if~then, when, logically, result in, so~that, as, aftermath, inasmuch as, on account of, on the grounds, thence, therefrom, thereupon, to that end, whence, wherefore, forasmuch as, ergo, hence, as long as

One thing you need to be aware of is that among these, they are placed in different order.

> A. therefore, thus : cause+therefore+effect
> B. because, since, for, as : effect+because+cause

When you see these, expect a logical cause or outcome.

3. _____ for his hideous crimes, the _____ arguably deserved capital punishment.

(A) Recognized..minor
(B) Famous..superstar
(C) Oblivious..malefactor
(D) Disreputable..victim
(E) Notorious..felon

In this question, the first blank should be filled in with a word like "famous." Then the word for the second blank should be something whose crime deserves heavy consequences such as death penalty. Since the person has a bad reputation, the person should be a felon. This is the type of causality question where the signal is hidden. The causality signal will appear only when you rephrase it like the following.

->Since (As/Because) the man was notorious for his crimes, he deserves capital punishment.

Therefore, the answer is E.

Categorization & List Signals

Here is a list of words that represent "categorization" o r "list"

moreover, furthermore, also, additionally, in addition, besides, by the same token, further, likewise, more, as well, simultaneously, else, along with

These words signal that two or more concepts or items are existent. The two items could be of equal value/status or one could be better/worse than the other. Very often, these are compared or related.

4. Even more financially _____ than his latest bestsellers is his debut book: Rich Dad and Poor Dad.

(B) profound (B) sound (C) naive (D) ineffectual
(E) unproductive

The word that best fits the blank should have the meaning, "successful," so the closest answer is B.

Examples and Details

Here is a list of words that represent "example"

illustrate, example, exemplify, paragon, model, archetype, prototype, classic, facsimile, imitation, typical, representative, standard, atypical, imperfect, epitomize, exhibit, fly speck, precedent, pattern, representation, stereotype, specimen, sampling, symbol, icon, yardstick, benchmark, exemplar, case history, case in point, proof, touchstone, paradigm, norm, measure, canon, embodiment, incarnation, quintessence, realization, reification, apotheosis, avatar, cast, conformation, embracement, instance, mirror, figure, portrait, portrayal, idol, fetish, replica, reproduction, similitude, statue, dead ringer, carbon copy, copy, figurine, manikin, marionette, puppet, presentiment, ringer, spectacle, tableau, twin, vignette, treatise, item, engraving

5. Since one of the design for the upcoming fashion show wa s stolen, the designer had to go through all of his past works to gather ideas for a new _____.

(A) nicety (B) stipulation (C) paragon (D) bargain (E) prototy pe

For this particular question, you need to be familiar with designer vocabulary. A "design" is just a drawing whereas a "prototype" is the actual rendition (realization) of it. In other words, it is the real thing. For the blank, we need a word that is similar to "sample" or a real object created after the conceptual drawing of it. Therefore, the answer is E.

Here is a list of words that represent "detail"

minute, miniscule, myopic, provincial, nebulous, myriad, countless, immeasurable, calculated, infinite, multiple, bilingual, multilingual, nuance, accessory, cue, peculiarity, component, specification, trivial, nuts and bolts, factor, minutia, nicety, nitty-gritty, brass tacks, article, analyze, catalog, circumstantiate, delineate, depict, describe, designate, elaborate, embellish, enumerate, spell out, stipulate, summarize, sweat details, uncover, misrepresent, effigy, statuette, torso, diagram, sketch, puny, scanty, scrubby, slight, trifling, bitty, cramped, diminutive, humble, inconsequential, microscopic, miniature, minuscule, paltry, petite, petty, picayune, inconsiderable, limited, dwarf, midget, stingy, stringent, parsimonious, miserly, skimping, thrifty, penny-pinching, tight-wad, frugal, meager, methodical, niggardly, penurious, provident, prudent

6. The doctor approved of Myra's leave only after giving her nurse _____ instructions on the patient's medication, physical therapy, and check-ups.

(A) banal (B) redundant (C)specific (D) limited
(E) magnanimous

Here, the doctor seems to be a very meticulous (detail-oriented) person as he/she checks on almost everything. However, there is no negative meaning attached to it. Therefore, the answer should be C.

Here is a list of words that represent "large" or "big"

ample, bulky, burly, capacious, colossal, commodious, considerable, cornucopia, immense, husky, hulking, hefty, massive, oversized, packed, ponderous, substantial, stuffed, strapping, whopper, voluminous, whopping, sizable, magnanimous, generous, spendthrift, improvident

7. The advertising campaign for the new theme park was a ____ ____; it was costly, mistargeted, and unappealing

(A) blunder (B) fiasco (C) success (D) affliction (E) boon

Here, the ad campaign was a failure. Since "blunder" means a minor mistake, it can't be the answer. Moreover, there are a number of clues after the semi-colon that hint us that the ad campaign was, not a small one, but a <u>big failure</u>. So the answer is B.

The Expected

There are words that hint you to expect something that is obvious. Here is the list.

apparent, obvious, clearly, absolute, vivid, definite, evid ent, tangible, substantial, discernible, marked, noticeable , perceivable, sensible, significant, negligible, apprehend, suspect, assume, conjecture, contemplate, deliberate, pr esume, surmise, envisage, forecast, figure, presuppose, c oming, conventional, habitual, planned for, prophesize, anticipate, premeditated,

8. It was obvious that the newly recruited soccer player would increase the team morale; he was truly more than a _____.

(A) transaction (B) loss   (C) solution   (D) envoy
(E) surrogate

Since it was guaranteed that the new recruit would be a plus to the team, he was more than just mediocre (meaning: not so great, so so). However, the expression "truly more than" is a hidden negative word. Therefore, the answer has to be something mediocre. So the answer is E.

The Unexpected

There are words that hint you to expect something unexpected. Here is the list.

surprisingly, amazingly, shockingly, astound, awe, daze, dazzle, startle, striking, stun, ironic, anomaly, odd, abrupt, prodigious, staggering, swift, unanticipated, unforeseen, unheralded, electrifying, eye-opening, fortuitous, haphazard, random, impulsive, impetuous, instantaneous, impromptu, extemporaneous, out of the blue, accidental, arbitrary, casual, erratic, fluke, reckless, unconscious, desultory, devil-may-care, helter-skelter, indiscriminate, offhand, slapdash, slipshod, spontaneous, aimless, disorderly, unpremeditated, willy-nilly

9. The judges at the speech contest was amazed to see such touching speech delivered by a _____.

(A) fledgling (B) guru (C) connoisseur (D) veteran (E) pundit

Unlike their expectations, the judges were amazed at the result. Therefore, the speaker must have been a real beginner. Therefore, the answer to this question is A.

READING
2. SENTENCE COMPLETION QUESTIONS 2

How well did you do on the previous section? I hope you did well on them.

On the next page is another set of Sentence Completion Questions. Again, work on them for 5-10 minutes and then go through the following explanations.

Sentence Completion Question Set 2

10. A substance added to create a chemical reaction is called a _____ ; without this particular agent, nothing happens.

(A) compound (B) catalyst (C) solution (D) conundrum
(E) mixture

11. Dr. Jones was so _____ a physician that he never _____ his duty for the past decade.

(A) devoted..encounter
(B) lackadaisical..eschew
(C) dedicated..shirk
(D) easy-going..malinger
(E) meticulous..face

12. The challenger to the incumbent officer won most of his supporters when he hit back his carping opponent with _____.

(A) aggression (B) common sense (C) repartee (D) diatribe (E) idiocy

13. Martha _____ to court after the jury found her guilty.

(A) charged (B) appealed (C) litigated (D) summoned
(E) affronted

14. The international court judges thought that the _____ attitudes of the emissaries from both countries were not _____ to the case at hand.

(A) belligerent..harmful
(B) biting..helpful

(C) wrathful..problematic
(D) amicable..beneficial
(E) diplomatic..advantageous

15. The nurse applied ointment to the abrasion to _____ the wounded soldier's pain.

(A) upset (B) exaggerate (C) escalate (D) leave (E) ease

16. The nuns didn't agree with their head priest that anything that he said would _____ God's words in the bible.

(A) complement   (B) appoint to (C) equate to (D) counter (E) resemble

17. The rising _____ between the cliques would never _____ as long as their healthcare bill is on the table.

(A) conflict..penetrate
(B) contention..be construed
(C) encounter..be solved
(D) feud..cease
(E) clash..be reckoned

18. The fire marshal concluded that the conflagration was a _____: the janitor apparently misinterpreted the sign that said, "inflammable."

(A) mishap   (B) arson   (C) anomaly (D) mystery
(E) bonus

Colons (:) and Semi-colons (;)

In sentence completion questions, both colons and semi-colons are used in similar fashion. We will go into their uses when we cover grammar (Ch.24) In this section, we will just say that everything before or after a colon or semi-colon are basically the same.

Ex) I didn't do it; somebody else must have done it.

Here, "I didn't do it" means that "somebody else must have done it."

I didn't do it=Somebody else did it.

10. A substance added to create a chemical reaction is called a _____ ; without this particular agent, nothing happens.

(A) compound (B) catalyst (C) solution (D) conundrum
(E) mixture

This is like the 20 questions or the crossword puzzle, right? What is a substance that is added to create a chemical reaction? The answer is B. The key is the part after the semi-colon, "without this particular agent, nothing happens."

Two Blanks

In two blank questions, simply work on one side and work on the other.

11. Dr. Jones was so _____ a physician that he has never _____ his duty for the past decade.

(A) devoted..encountered
(B) lackadaisical..eschewed
(C) dedicated..shirked

(D) easy-going..malingered
(E) meticulous..faced

First, analyze what the author is trying to say. It seems like the physician was such a diligent person that he always showed up at work for the last decade. A list of potential candidates for the first blank is "diligent," "dedicated," "devoted." Then the suitable for the second blank is to "avoid" or "evade," because there is that negative word, "never." Therefore, the answer is C.

Commonly Appearing Vocabulary

Few of the most commonly appearing vocabulary on tests are words that mean "agree," "to criticize," "to object" "bitter," "important," "soothe," "relate," "compare," "problem," and "solution." After all, aren't these what we educated people do all the time? We agree, criticize or object to things, make bitter comments, soothe people, judge the importance of something, relate and compare things, discuss problems and solutions.

Criticize, Irritate, Bitter, and Soothe

Here is a list of words that means "to criticize"

disapprove, bash, blame, blister, carp, castigate, censure, chastise, chide, condemn, denounce, denunciate, renounce, disparage, excoriate, fluff, fulminate against, fustigate, lambaste, nit-pick, pan, reprimand, reprobate, reprove, scathe, slam

12. The challenger to the incumbent officer won most of his supporters when he hit back his carping opponent with _____.

(A) aggression (B) common sense (C) repartee (D) diatribe (E) idiocy

What are some of the qualities do voters wish to see in a political candidate? Probably "honesty" "humor" "intelligence" would be few of them. It would be boring to beat your opponent by doing what your opponent is doing: criticizing the enemy. Instead, if you can respond back to criticism with wit almost instinctively, you will easily outshine the person. Such an expression is "repartee," C.

Here is a list of words that mean "irritate" or "offend"

irritate, irksome, abrade, affront, aggravate, annoy, bug, chafe, distemper, drive up the wall, enrage, exasperate, fret, gall, get on the nerve, get under the skin, grate, harass, incense, inflame, infuriate, madden, nettle, provoke, pester, pique, rankle, rasp, rattle, rile, roil, ruffle, sour, vex, accuse, appeal, beseech, charge, claim, contest, enter a plea, file suit, litigate, drag into court, take into court, haul into court, institute legal proceedings, petition, plead, prosecute, solicit, summon, supplicate, requisition, renounce, urge

13. Martha _____ to court after the jury found her guilty.

(A) charged   (B) appealed   (C) litigated   (D) summoned
(E) affronted

Since Martha was found guilty, she is not just summoned (called upon) or simply charged with a crime. What do you think she would do next? Appealing to court would be her next step, right? So, the answer is B.

Here is a list of words that mean "bitter"

acerbic, bitter, cutting, biting, caustic, mordant, nasty,
stinging, trenchant, vitriolic, acrimonious, belligerent,
censorious, churlish, crabby, cranky, indignant, irascible,
peevish, petulant, rancorous, spiteful, wrathful,
begrudging, incisive, embittered, fierce, irreconcilable,
resentful, sardonic, sour, sore, sullen, virulent,
cantankerous, carping, caviling, nagging, testy, scathing,
blunt, brusque, captious, choleric, surly, sulky, sullen,
tart, snappy, saturnine, prickly, splenetic, grouchy,
crotchety, crusty, acidic

14. The international court judges thought that the
_____ attitudes of the emissaries from both countries
were not _____ to the case at hand.

(F) belligerent..harmful
(G) biting..helpful
(H) wrathful..problematic
(I) amicable..beneficial
(J) diplomatic..advantageous

The first blank should be filled in with a word that
means "hostile." And since such "not so friendly attitudes"
are not improving the situation, the word for the second
blank should mean, "worsening." However, don't forget the
negative word, "not," which turns the answer into something
positive (or helpful). So, the answer should be B.

Here is a list of words that mean "to soothe"

allay, alleviate, appease, assuage, balm, becalm, cheer,
composure, lighten, hush, lull, mitigate, numb, mollify,
pacify, path things ups, ointment, relieve, settle,
smooth, subdue, tranquil, soothe

15. The nurse applied ointment to the abrasion to _____
the wounded soldier's pain.

(A) upset (B) exaggerate (C) escalate (D) leave (E) ease

What does an ointment do to scars? It relieves pain. So, the answer is E.

Relations, Comparisons, and Correlations

Here is a list of words that mean relations, comparisons, and correlations.

collate, compare, commensurate, equate, emulate, equipoise, measure up, run abreast, symmetric, asymmetrical, equivalent, invariable, identical, indistinguishable, tantamount, egalitarian, duplicate, scan, assess, segregate, scrutinize, examine, probe, monitor, neglect, analogy, allegory, recite, relate, pertain, allocate, appoint, commission, affiliation, affinity, alliance, association, consanguinity, kin, kindred, kinship, liaison, propinquity, sibling, relative, coalition, accord, betrothal, bond, coherence, collaboration, collusion, scheme, communion, compact, concord, concurrence, confederation, congruity, conjunction, entente, federation, fraternization, interrelation, matrimony, mutuality, pact, tie, treaty, hostility, estrangement, discord, correspondence, alternation, complement, equivalence, homology, parallel, resemblance, semblance, connotation, juxtaposition, concomitance, concordance, train of thought,

16. The nuns didn't agree with their head priest that anything that he said would _____ God's words in the bible.

(A) complement (B) appoint to (C) equate to (D) counter (E) resemble

The nuns think that their head priest should not play God. Therefore, they do not treat his words with God's. The answer is C.

Problems and Solutions

Here is a list of words that mean "problem"

complication, dilemma, dispute, mess, obstacle, predicament, quandary, struggle, torment, woe, concern, hot water, hindrance, distress, grief, bustle, exasperation, flurry, fuss, molestation, nudge, nuisance, pain, perplexity, pest, plague, pother, strain, vexation, conflict, impasse, mire, clash, collision, contention, fracas, strife, tug of war, brawl, contend, run against tide, tangle, skirmish, melee, animosity, hostility, barrage, assault, carnage, rampage, encounter, havoc, scrimmage, agitation, broil, foe, formidable, feud, grapple, wrangle, quarrel

Here is a list of words that mean "solution"

resolution, elucidation, explanation, clarification, explication, unravel, construe, vindication, interpretation, counterclaim, remark, repartee, rebuttal, illumination, enlighten, disentangle, fathom, crack, reckon, decipher, decode, decrypt, deduce, render

17. The rising _____ between the cliques would never _____ as long as their healthcare bill is on the table.

(A) conflict..penetrate
(B) contention..be construed
(C) encounter..be solved
(D) feud..cease
(E) clash..be reckoned

Two parties are fighting over the healthcare bill. Therefore, the word for the first blank should be a synonym of "conflict" and the one for the second blank should be "to stop," unless the negotiation is over. Therefore, the answer is D.

Confusing Words & Signals

In fact/Indeed vs. but, flammable vs. inflammable, virtually, condescending, usually, patronize vs. patron, compact vs. compound, organization vs. organism are confusing to readers.

18. The fire marshall concluded that the conflagration was a _____: the janitor apparently misinterpreted the sign that said, "inflammable."

(A) mishap   (B) arson   (C) anomaly   (D) mystery
(E) bonus

Since the janitor obviously read the sign wrong, "inflammable," the case must be an accident. Therefore, the answer should be A.

*For additional information on the idea relationships or sentential relationships, read Chapter five and six.

READING
3. 5 TYPES OF WRITING

The first thing you need to know when you start reading is what kind of text you are dealing with. I am going to list five: descriptive, narrative, argumentative (persuasive), explanatory, and expository (See Table 1).

A descriptive writing is a writing that describes a state, event, or a process. Even though it is mainly used to describe a fixed state where time doesn't flow, it is also used to describe an event or a process (time flows). An example of a descriptive writing is a news report of an accident (e.g. 120 people got killed at a plane crash last night.). There is no change in the character or reader's attitude. Therefore no morals or lessons. Simply something unexpected happened. However, this type of writing is common in short passage questions.

The second type of writing is narrative. In a narrative, there is usually a time flow. It is basically a story where readers expect a change. The change could be in the characters' attitude, in the setting, or even in the readers' minds. Skillful writers make this transition very smooth and logical and everything makes sense as we move towards the

		Descriptive	-to describe a state, event or a process (changes in states).
▼ ▼ ▼ Evolution, Complication, Condensation, Nominalization ▼ ▼ ▼	Conclusion last (hidden)	Narrative	-to explain an event or a process (change) through descriptions of who did what, where, when, why, and how (characters/environment). -time flow: time signaling adverbs (yesterday, today, one day, tomorrow) or changed time orders -change in the participants' attitude: the author, the characters
	Conclusion first	Argumentative/ Persuasive	-to argue that one idea is better than the other. -argument and supports (evidence/reasons) -logical flow: nominalization, categorization -time flow: process or procedure
		Explanatory	-to explain a concept or a social, political or scientific event. -definition: explanation of new or difficult concepts, usually at the beginning. -logical flow: nominalization, categorization -time flow: process or procedure
		Expository (complex: arguments backed up by explanations)	-to explain ideas and argue that one is better than the other (or explain why both are good or necessary). -definition: explanation of new or difficult concepts, usually at the beginning. -argument and supports (evidence/reasons) -logical flow: nominalization, categorization -time flow: process or procedure

end. Another notable characteristic of this type of writing is that a narrative can have different phases (or stages) and these can be easily identified by time markers (e.g. yesterday, today, first, second, etc.). Here, time is important because the story develops as time goes.

Table 1. 5 Types of Writing

The third type is Argumentative writing. It is a form that we use to argue or persuade the reader. Unlike narrative, it has a logical flow instead of time flow. This means that there is the author's argument and his/her supports. First, the author makes an argument and provides evidence and examples to prove that he/she is right. So, here, time will not solve anything here and it doesn't matter. Instead, logic matters.

The fourth type of writing is called, "Explanatory." Some scholars do not distinguish explanatory writing from expository writing, but I do here because the distinction is quite useful in language testing. For example, most TOEFL reading passages are not really "expository," as they are mainly written to explain a concept or phenomena. In other words, the authors simply try to explain things to readers. He/she will provide definitions, descriptions, and categorizations, but not many arguments. Most of the content in an explanatory are generally accepted concepts or theories, so they are hard to be refuted anyway.

The last type of writing is called, "Expository." Most SAT, LSAT, GRE reading passages belong to this. Here, the author usually deals with a controversial topic and this can confuse the readers in two ways. First, the author may discuss a difficult topic and may give readers a hard time. Second, the author may present two or more arguments and confuse the readers. There can be double passages, which we will deal with later, and some quote experts in the field (see expert table) to strengthen their arguments or belittle the opposite side. What's even worse? Some even change positions as they write!

Can all the writings in the testing world be classified as these five? I'd say somewhat. We certainly can't list all the writings types in all tests. Moreover, highly skilled writers or experts in a field mix these different types. In other words, in more challenging tests, there can be cross-over writings that start with a personal anecdote, explain difficult concepts, compare/contrast different theories, and end with an open thought.

However, making a note of these distinctions can surely help, because with this particular piece of knowledge, we can trace the authors' thoughts more accurately, recognize turns, and ultimately score higher on the test.

So, I'd say we are off a good start, right?

READING
4. PURPOSE, PARTICIPANTS, AND CONTEXT

Miller (1984) emphasized the importance of purpose, p articipants, and context in any kind of text analysis. I, too, be lieve that these are important things to consider in understan ding the reading passages because they help us imagine the p hysical situation that the author is describing in our own min ds.

Purpose-what is the purpose of this writing?
Participants (who is writing to whom?)
Context (under what situation and in what style?).

Now, let's go into detail.

1) *What is the purpose of the writing?*
   What is the author's argument?
   What does the author want to say?
   Why does the author say/write this?
   What/why does the character do this?

In George Orwell's "The Animal Farm," the message wou

ld be political (dictatorship/totalitarianism), whereas Henrik Ibsen's "A Doll's House," the message is related to women's limited role in society.

2) *Who is writing to whom?*
   Who is the writer? What is he/she? Where does he/she come from?
   Who is the reader/audience? What is he/she? Where does he/she come from?
   To whom is the character writing this letter? What is the relationship between characters?

   In a narrative, think of why A is saying something to B. " What does it mean when he/she says this?" is a common question on standardized tests. In order to find the answer, you have to understand the relationships between characters and their situations (see next)

3) *Under what situation and in what style (genre) is the author writing?*
   What is the author's/reader's situation?
   What is the style (genre) of writing (narrative/exposition)?
   What is the situation/background of the character (s)?

   There is always a reason why a writer chooses to write in a specific genre. Find out that reason as they might be helpful in understanding the motive behind writing the text.
   Purpose, participants, and context will guide you through the text and help you answer these questions. They are as follows.

   Organization: What is the function of paragraph 3 in the passage?
   Purpose: Why does the author respond this way?
   Purpose: Why does the author quote _____?
   Context: What is the tone of the author?

Depending on purpose, participants, and context of the st ory, the author may suggest the conclusion (argument) first (argumentative, and expository) or the process first (narrative, descriptive).

1) Brad and Angelina broke up after they have been living to gether for Six years.

2) Brad and Angelina have been living together happily in th e same house with their children for six years until they offici ally broke up yesterday.

Genre Distinctions

In some writings, genre distinctions are clear, but in oth ers, genre distinctions are unclear. Thus, one should carefully analyze the following signals in the text to find the hidden ar guments.

READING
5. EIGHTEEN IDEA RELATION SIGNALS

Pitkin (1973) is known for his study of idea relationships. Why do we need to know these to improve our reading? Because they are the very framework of our common mindsets. Especially in our modern world, these eighteen elements are pretty much all we talk about everyday. We argue with each other, talk about the possibilities of getting things done, talk about our expectations and surprises, discuss the significance/insignificance of something, analyze the cause and effect, correlations (how things are related), validity (truthfulness/usefulness), and reliability(how dependable it is), changes, manners, time, locations,…and etc. In other words these are the essential tools in our scientific, logical, and emotional thinking. For our purpose they are useful tools in understanding the science, history, and literature texts.

In this book, I will first explain these logical relationships (Chapter 3 and 4). That way when you read any kind of text, you will not miss these important signals. Main ideas and most important test questions all come out where are located. These are the signals that help you recognize what you shouldn't miss to get the questions right and ultimately score high on the test. So, let's go through them now.

1) Argument (strongest)-<u>A is B, all, everything, universally, always</u>

2) Possibility (second strongest) or expected (modality): <u>can, may, possible, certainly, surely, some, generally.</u>

3) Unexpected: <u>surprising, amazing, or shocking, ironical</u>. Expect unusual results.

4) Significant: <u>important, essential, necessary, factor, variable</u>

5) Not significant: <u>unnecessary, meaningless, unimportant, regardless.</u> The variable at hand is unimportant.

6) Cause and Effect (causality): <u>therefore, thus</u> (cause+therefore+effect), <u>because, since, for, as</u> (effect+because+cause), <u>aftermath</u>.

7) Correlation: <u>A is related to B, A is pertinent to B</u>. Two or more things are not necessarily in cause & effect relationship, but are positively or negatively inter-related with one another.

8) Support: <u>and, furthermore, additionally, moreover, also, in addition, not only~but also.</u> Here, an additional idea(s) is added or the issue is further analyzed. Alternatively, the degree of something either increases or decreases.

9) Contrastive: <u>however, but, although, even though, nevertheless</u>. The argument takes a partial/complete turn and many questions are asked around this.

10) Change of Subject/Step: <u>before, next, the following</u>. Previous discussion is over and a new concept is introduced.

11) Purpose/intention (why): <u>in order to, to, because, for.</u> These explain why the author/character thinks or takes action.

12) Method (how): <u>how to, by, through.</u> These explain how the author/character takes/took action.

13) Comparative-<u>rank higher/lower/finest/worst</u>

14) Time/locational order-sequential, synchronous, reverse time order.

15) Linear-General to specific (deductive)/specific to general (inductive)

16) Manner-<u>A is angry/A is sarcastic</u>

17) Affective (change)-<u>A influences B or A becomes B.</u>

18) Degree-<u>A changes B little/much/slightly</u>.

Don't think of these as independent signals as they often appear with others in mixed forms. For example, "Manner" will appear with "affective" in a question asking if there is a change in the character's attitude. In another question, you would be asked to find the author's argument and the key to that answer would be the contrastive signal. Practice identifying different idea relationships when you read texts.

READING
6. ELEVEN IDEA SEQUENCES

Pitkin (1973) also came up with eleven idea sequences. These are the some of the most common patterns found in an exposition.

1) General to Specific (deductive) and Specific to General (inductive)

These are the two most common sequences in most expository essays. It is also called a "linear" relationship.

If the conclusion comes first, then it is deductive. If the conclusion comes last, then it is inductive.

E.g. deductive: Korean students are great (generalization). First, they listen very well (specific 1). Second, they are very smart (specific 2). Third, they are always well-prepared (specific 3).

2) Cause to Effect/Effect to Cause

A causes B or B is caused by A. Either way works.

3) Chronological, Simultaneous, Reverse time order

Sometimes ideas can be presented according to time.

4) Problem to Solution/Solution to Problem

First a problem is presented and its solution is given. Sometimes a solution is given and further problems are noted.

5) High Ranked to Low Ranked/and Low Ranked to High Ranked

Ideas can be presented in hierarchies. They can be presented from top to bottom or vice versa. In other words, some ideas are subsidiaries (categories) of more important basic ideas.

Now, we have reviewed the Eighteen Idea Signals and Eleven Idea Signals. Your job is to practice identifying these in different texts. In the next two chapters, I will tell you how.

READING
7. NARRATIVE PASSAGE ANALYSIS

Purpose, Participants, and Context

Think about who is writing to whom, the main characters, and the event. If the story is too complicated for you, draw pictures, tables or write notes. Define their relationships. Are they friends, family, or coworkers? Think about what the major change or event that occurred in the story. How did people change after the event? How did they respond to the event? Whose attitude changed? Sometimes, the narrator's attitude changed. What is the environment that makes characters to act in such a way? To sum it up, two things.

1. Find out about the people, their relationships, and their situations
2. Look for changes.

Now, I am going to discuss how to do these two in a narrative text.

1. Read the Blurb

The italicized part of the passage that comes before the reading passage is called a "blurb." Often these blurbs can give you much information on the reading passage you are about to read; for example, the topic, the setting and the background of the story, the characters and their relationships and conflicts, and about their author.

2. Look for Sudden Changes

Sudden changes are easy to find as they stick out in the text. Some are in conversations (quotes) come, some appear with an exclamation point (!), and some appear in the beginning part of a paragraph. Some appear after a contrastive signal such as "but" or "however." Sometimes, you are expected to guess as you read along.

3. Look for Time Markers

Time markers or time adverbs represent time (See Table 1 in Chapter 1). Look for words like the following.

ex) yesterday, today, one day, tomorrow, next

Unlike the expository writing (See Chapter 1) the whole fun of reading a narrative is for the readers to find out. As long as we are normally functioning literate humans we can understand, think and find out about the plot. These time markers are road signs for you. Think about the small or sudden changes in between these time markers.

3. Pay Attention to the Conversations (or Quotes)

Whether a scientist writes about the universe or a Pulitzer prize winning novelist writes about the life in the concentration camp, a narrative passage has a personal voice. What this means is that everyone is biased in some way and the author or each character is trying to tell you (or the reader) about his/her thoughts and opinions.

4. Pay careful attention to the author's description

If the story is told in the first-person narrator form, pay attention to what the narrator talks about, how he talks about it, and how he responds to events. Since we are listening to one person talking about how he/she sees the world, shouldn't we all assume that he is biased to start with? You will eventually find out whether your doubt is right or wrong by reading along.

The next page is a narrative passage with questions. Work on them using the strategies you just learned.

Reading Comprehension Question Set 1
-Narrative

*The following passage is adaptea from a short story written in the 19ᵗʰce
ntury.*

Monsieur Chantal stopped. He was sitting on the edge of the
billiard table, his feet hanging, and was playing with a ball wit
h his left hand, while with his right he crumpled a rag which
served to rub the chalk marks from the slate. A little (5)red i
n the face, his voice thick, he was talking away to himself no
w, lost in his memories. After a slight pause he continued:
"By Jove! She was pretty at eighteen--and graceful--and perfe
ct. Ah! She was so sweet--and good and true--and (10)charmi
ng! She had such eyes- blue-transparent--clear--such eyes as I
have never seen since!"
I asked: "Why did she never marry?"
He answered, not to me, but to the word "marry" which had
caught his ear, "Why? why? She never would--she never (15)
would! She had a dowry of thirty thousand francs, and she re
ceived several offers--but she never would! She seemed sad a
t that time. That was when I married my cousin, little Charlot
te, my wife, to whom I had been engaged for six years."
(20)I looked at M. Chantal, and it seemed to me that I was lo
oking into his very soul, and I was suddenly witnessing one o
f those humble and cruel tragedies of honest, straightforward
, blameless hearts, one of those secret tragedies known to no
one, not even the silent and resigned (25)victims. A rash curi
osity suddenly impelled me to exclaim:
"You should have married her, Monsieur Chantal!"
He startled, looked at me, and said, "I? Marry whom?"
"Mademoiselle Pearl."
(30)"Why?"
"Because you loved her more than your cousin."
He stared at me with strange, round, bewildered eyes and sta
mmered, "I loved her--I? How? Who told you that?"
"Why, anyone can see that--and it's even on account of her (

37

(35) that you delayed for so long your marriage to your cousin who had been waiting for you for six years."

He dropped the ball which he was holding in his left hand, and, seizing the chalk rag in both hands, he buried his face in it and began to sob. He was weeping with his eyes, nose and (40) mouth in a heartbreaking yet ridiculous manner, like a sponge which one squeezes. I felt bewildered, ashamed; I wanted to run away, and I no longer knew what to say, do, or attempt.

Suddenly Madame Chantal's voice sounded on the stairs. (45) "Haven't you men almost finished smoking your cigars?"

I opened the door and cried: "Yes, madame, we are coming right down."

Then I rushed to her husband, and, seizing him by the shoulders, I cried: "Monsieur Chantal, my friend Chantal, (50) listen to me; your wife is calling; pull yourself together, we must go downstairs."

I caught him by the hands and dragged him into his bedroom, muttering: "I beg your pardon, I beg your pardon, Monsieur Chantal, for having caused you such sorrow--but--(55) I did not know--you--you understand."

He squeezed my hand, saying: "Yes--yes--there are difficult moments."

Then he plunged his face into a bowl of water. When he emerged from it he did not yet seem to me to be presentable; (60) but I thought of a little stratagem. As he was growing worried, looking at himself in the mirror, I said to him, "All you have to do is to say that a little dust flew into your eye and you can cry before everybody to your heart's content."

I went over to Mademoiselle Pearl and watched her, (65) tormented by an ardent curiosity, which was turning to positive suffering. She must indeed have been pretty, with her gentle, calm eyes, so large that it looked as though she never closed them like other mortals. Her gown was a little ridiculous, a real old maid's gown, which was unbecoming (70) without appearing clumsy.

"Mademoiselle Pearl" by Guy de Maupassant (1850-1893)

1. In line 13 ("He answered,…ear"), the author views Monsieur Chantal's reaction as

(A) peculiar

(B) expected

(C) erroneous

(D) thoughtful

(E) intelligible

2. The word "dowry" (line 15) most nearly means

(A) real estate

(B) status

(C) capital

(D) prospect

(E) alimony

3. In "You…Chantal!" (line 27), the narrator's attitude is best described as

(A) considerate

(B) vexing

(C) decadent

(D) whimsical

(E) aggravated

4. The author would most likely characterize the attitude of Monsieur Chantal "I loved…that?" (line 33) as

(A) pretentious

(B) modest

(C) secretive

(D) frustrated

(E) enchanted

5. Which of the following best describes the change in Monsieur Chantal's feeling from (line 1-6) to (line 37-43)

(A) fear to intrepid

(B) nostalgic to flustered

(C) sentimental to dreamy

(D) content to gloomy

(E) agitated to paranoia

6. "Haven't...cigars?" in line 45 serves to
(A) tell how much time has elapsed
(B) suggest the gentlemen to continue talking
(C) notify the Mademoiselle Pearl to get ready
(D) question if the gentlemen are really smoking cigars
(E) express Madame Chantal's anger towards her husband

7. In line 60 ("but...stratagem"), the author is in response to
(A) Madame Chantal's calling from downstairs
(B) Mademoiselle Pearl's torment
(C) Mademoiselle Pearl's difficult moments
(D) Monsieur Chantal's unpresentable appearance
(E) Monsieur Chantal's sudden burst into tears

8. Which of the following best describes the change in Mademoiselle Pearl's feeling, "I went...suffering." (line 64-66)
(A) nervous to nonchalant
(B) burdened to lighthearted
(C) diffident to confident
(D) tolerant to intolerant
(E) curious to suffering

9. The author's description of Mademoiselle Pearl's appearance in "She was... clumsy." (line 68-70) is
(A) cryptic
(B) derisive
(C) inexorable
(D) even-handed
(E) facetious

*Answers on page 190

READING
8. EXPOSITORY PASSAGE ANALYSIS

Purpose, Participants, and Context

Think about who is writing to whom, the main characters, and the event. If the story is too complicated for you, draw pictures, tables or write notes. Define their relationships. Are they friends, family, or coworkers? Think about what the major change or event that occurred in the story. How did people change after the event? How did they respond to the event? Whose attitude changed? Sometimes, the narrator's attitude changed. What is the environment that makes characters to act in such a way? To sum it up, two things.

1. Find out about the people, their relationships, and their situations
2. Look for changes.

Now, I am going to discuss how to do these two in a narrative text.

1. Read the Blurb

The italicized part of the passage that comes before the reading passage is called a "blurb." Often these blurbs can give you much information on the reading passage you are about to read; for example, the topic, the history of the conflict/controversy (e.g. when global warming started), the relationships between two or more groups/individuals, and about the author (s).

2. Time Flow VS. Logical Flow

Sudden changes are easy to find as they stick out in the text. Some are in conversations (quotes) come, some appear with an exclamation point (!), and some appear in the beginning part of a paragraph. Sometimes, you are expected to guess as you read along.

3. Look for Arguments

There are several ways to find arguments. Although not all of them are all important arguments, they are noteworthy as many questions are created around these points.

1. Look where arguments are likely appear like the very beginning (location).
2. The main argument often appears after contrastive signals such as "but" and "however."
3. Look right before where examples or specific details are given.
4. If the claim is too hard to understand, then try to understand the author's point through his examples, illustrations, and demonstrations.
5. Find categorization signals such as "moreover," or "in addition." This means, there are at least two or

more specific points and right before these, there is an argument.

6. Some are presented in the form of a question. If you think of a logical answer, that is the argument.

7. Sometimes no argument or main idea is explicitly stated. You simply have to summarize and take a guess.

8. Nominalizations (names a controversial topic such as abolitionism), abstractions and generalizations can hint at claims.

9. Locate supports and evidences. These usually entail an argument.

10. Look for modality (modal verbs such as may, could, and etc.) as they represent, judgment, possibility, necessity, and request.

11. Arguments are repeated many times throughout the essay.

4. Look for Contrastive Signals

You need to pay close attention to contrastive signals as these signal the turn or change in the author's argument.

The Author   You

The author has made a turn in his argument, but if you continue to go the same direction, you are unlikely to get the question right.

Quickly browse through the whole text looking for "but," and "however." If there is no contrastive signals, there is no turn; the author's argument is consistent throughout.

5. Pay Attention to Categories & Distinctions

Here are some of the notable features of expository texts.

1. Categorization: the # of different kinds
2. Definition: ideas defined toward one or more sides
3. Comparison/Contrast: compare and contrast two or more things
4. Factor/Significance/Insignificance: Analyze the validity and reliability of a factor that influences the result.
5. Abstractions/Nominalizations: special terms coined to deal with the topic more efficiently (e.g.

Locate these in the text, mark them or write them down. Use them to understand the author's argument and supports as these show you the depth and width of the topic. They help you focus on the topic by showing you the topical boundaries. This way, you don't make a baseless claim or jump to conclusions.

6. Author's Attitude and Use of Quotations

In expository texts, finding out the author's tone of voice or attitude toward a topic or an argument is very important. In case you misunderstand or have difficulty understanding the author's position, try to have a large set of vocabulary with you before the time of actual testing.

Also, evaluate the author's attitude towards quotations and how he uses the quotations. Even if you fail to understand the author's argument, you may guess the author's point through his treatment of the quotation (i.e. he may criticize the quote or praise it).

The next page is an expository passage with questions. Work on them using the strategies you just learned.

Reading Comprehension Question Set 2
-Expository

The following passage was excerpted from a book written by a 19th Century American Author. He discusses a way of protest to the government.

I meet this American government, or its representative, the State government, directly, and face to face, once a year — no more — in the person of its tax-gatherer. My civil neighbor, the tax-gatherer, is the very man I have to deal (5)with — for it is, after all, with men and not with parchment that I quarrel — and he has voluntarily chosen to be an agent of the government. How shall he ever know well what he is and does as an officer of the government, or as a man, until he is obliged to consider whether he shall treat me, (10)his neighbor, for whom he has respect, as a neighbor and well-disposed man, or as a maniac and disturber of the peace, and see if he can get over this obstruction to his neighborliness without a ruder and more impetuous thought or speech corresponding with his action? I know this well, (15)that if one thousand, if one hundred, if ten men whom I could name — if ten honest men only — ay, if one HONEST man, in this State of Massachusetts, ceasing to hold slaves, were actually to withdraw from this co-partnership, and be locked up in the county jail therefore, it (20)would be the abolition of slavery in America. For it matters not how small the beginning may seem to be: what is once well done is done forever.

Under a government which imprisons any unjustly, the true place for a just man is also a prison. The proper place (25)to-day, the only place which Massachusetts has provided for her freer and less desponding spirits, is in her prisons, to be put out and locked out of the State by her own act, as they have already put themselves out by their principles. It is there that the fugitive slave, and the Mexican prisoner on (30)parole, and the Indian come to plead the wrongs of his race, should find them; on that separate, but more free and honorable ground, where the State places those who are not with her, but against her — the only house in a slave State in which a free man can abide with honor. If any think that (35)their influence would be lost there, and their voices no longer afflict the ear of the State, that they would not be as an enemy within its walls, they do not know by how much truth is stronger than error, nor how much more eloquently and effectively he can combat injustice who has experienced (40)a little in his own person. Cast your whole vote, not a strip of paper merely, but your whole influence. A minority is powerless while it conforms to the majority; it is not even a minority then; but it is irresistible when it clogs by its whole weight. If the alternative is to keep all just men in (45)prison, or give up war and slavery, the State will not hesitate which to choose. If a thousand men were not to pay their tax-bills this year, that would not be a violent and bloody measure, as it would be to pay them, and enable the State to commit violence and shed innocent blood. This is, (50)in fact, the definition of a peaceable revolution, if any such is possible. If the tax-gatherer, or any other public officer, asks me, as one has done, "But what shall I do?" my answer is, "If you really wish to do anything, resign your office." When the subject has refused allegiance, and the (55)officer has resigned his office, then the revolution is accomplished. But even suppose blood should flow. Is there not a sort of bloodshed when the conscience is wounded? Through this wound a man's real manhood and immortality flow out, and he bleeds to an everlasting death. I see this (60)blood flowing now.

When I converse with the freest of my neighbors, I perceive that, whatever they may say about the magnitude and seriousness of the question, and their regard for the public tranquility, the long and the short of the matter is, (65)that they cannot spare the protection of the existing government, and they dread the consequences to their property and families of disobedience to it. For my own part,

I should not like to think that I ever rely on the protection of the State. But, if I deny the authority of the State when it (70)presents its tax-bill, it will soon take and waste all my property, and so harass me and my children without end. This is hard. This makes it impossible for a man to live honestly, and at the same time comfortably in outward (75)respects. It will not be worth the while to accumulate property; that would be sure to go again. You must hire or squat somewhere, and raise but a small crop, and eat that soon. You must live within yourself, and depend upon yourself always tucked up and ready for a start, and not have (80)many affairs. A man may grow rich in a country even, if he will be in all respects a good subject of the government. Confucius said, "If a state is governed by the principles of reason, poverty and misery are subjects of shame; if a state is not governed by the principles of reason, riches and (85)honors are the subjects of shame." No: until I want the protection of Massachusetts to be extended to me in some distant Southern port, where my liberty is endangered, or until I am bent solely on building up an estate at home by peaceful enterprise, I can afford to refuse allegiance to (90)Massachusetts, and her right to my property and life. It costs me less in every sense to incur the penalty of disobedience to the State than it would to obey. I should feel as if I were worth less in that case.

From "Civil Disobedience" by Henry David Thoreau

1. In "if…America. " (line 16-20) the author is making a claim that
(A) one honest man may not be enough, but ten or more men can make a reform overnight.
(B) years of work in legislature is required to amend any unjust law such as slavery.
(C) if one man shows a good example by going to jail, he can make an immediate change that is more effective than years of work.

(D) any righteous movement may require both honest and dishonest people.
(E) a non-violent reform can be easily made all the time by one honest man spending a night in the county jail.

2. In "Under...prison. " (line 23-24) the author assumes that
(A) Massachusetts was a freer place before
(B) Massachusetts is doing something wrong
(C) he is treated justly
(D) he is an honest man
(E) the proper place for a just man is outside prison

3. In "The proper…prisons. " (line 24-26) the author is using a(n)
(A) analogy
(B) paradox
(C) simile
(D) personification
(E) metaphor

4. In "they…error." (line 37-38) the author is doing which of the following?
(A) justifying his previous statement
(B) criticizing those who fail to acknowledge their power
(C) questioning the significance of an issue
(D) setting up a principle
(E) giving a definition of a concept

5. Which of the following is most similar to the case described in "If...blood." (line 44-49)
(A) A group of congressmen who gain enough votes to impeach the president
(B) A general who successfully gains control of the government through a military coup d'état
(C) A group of union workers that achieves a pay raise after a peaceful strike

(D) A lawyer who wins a lawsuit against a company that is responsible for environmental pollution for the victims and himself

(E) A civil rights leader who persuades his followers to arm themselves and fight against government authorities

6. In "This…possible," (line 49-51), the author is
(A) self-contradicting himself
(B) providing an example
(C) proving a point
(D) making a hypothetical claim
(E) redefining the concept of peaceable revolution

7. In "If….office." (line 53-54), the author is
(A) blackmailing the public officer
(B) denying the alternative solution
(C) making a suggestion
(D) requesting the public officer to make an immediate choice
(E) reading the public officer's rights

8. In line 62, the word, "magnitude" most nearly means
(A) sequence
(B) extent
(C) insignificance
(D) maximum
(E) location

9. Which of the following statements, if true, would most weaken the author's statement in "if…end." (line 69-71)
(A) The State refuses to collect taxes when it cannot provide protection to its citizens

(B) The State only taxes those who practice their rights regularly.

(C) The State harasses non-tax payers on regular basis.

(D) The State no longer presents its tax-bill to the descendents of non-tax payers once their non-tax paying ancestors are deceased.

(E) The State guarantees unequal rights and protection to tax-paying and non-taxpaying citizens.

10. Which of the following statements, if true, would most strengthen the author's statement in "A man...government" (line 80-81)

(A) All the rich men in the country are neither corrupt nor good subjects to the government.

(B) The most corrupt men cannot be rich in the country.

(C) Only non-corrupt people can be citizens in the country.

(D) Not all the rich men in the country are good subjects to the government.

(E) The country has been reported to be indeed one of the most corrupt nations on the news for many years in a row.

11. In "Confucius...shame." (line 82-85) the author is using a quote

(A) to borrow authority

(B) to refute the previous claim

(C) to suggest an alternative solution to the problem

(D) to digress from the topic

(E) to make a point

*Answers on page 190

READING
9. QUESTION TYPE-1

For the next six chapters, I will review different kinds of reading question types. Learn to recognize them and put these theories into practice.

Connect the Reading Passage+Question+Answer

The reading passage, the question, and the answer together represent a uniform idea and help the reader understand the author's message.

1) Connect the reading passage and the question.
2) Connect the reading passage and the answer.
3) Connect the question and answer.

If you are pondering over two or three answer choices, then, connect the question and answer and see which one makes most sense.

For example, if answer choice (a) and (b) are attractive to you, then write as the following:

(a) Q)----------------------------Ans)-----------------------
(b) Q)----------------------------Ans)-----------------------

Doing this will help you see the distinctions more clearly. This technique is also very handy in grammar questions.

1. The Main Argument Questions

1) The main argument is repeated throughout the passage. Carefully read and re-read the parts that seem important.

2) For narrative, look for time markers (e.g. one day, suddenly, etc.) and look for changes in the author's attitude.

3) For exposition,
   a. Look for "but" or its variants. The main argument usually comes after "but" or around "but."

   b. Look for the following sentence types.

   -A is B or A does B. ex) John is a thief.
   -A sentence with action verb. ex) John steals things.
   -A sentence with modality. ex) John could be a thief.

2. The Author's Idea Questions

If you find the author's argument(s), write it down somewhere or mark it (them).

1) You will be asked to use the author's argument many times.
2) If there are two passages, you will be asked to compare and contrast the arguments.

3) You will be asked to strengthen or weaken the author's arguments.

4) You will be asked to find an analogy that is similar to the author's argument.

You don't have to read the whole passage to figure out the main idea.

1) Read the blurb before each passage (that is italicized).

2) Read the introduction. Both narrative essays and expository essays usually have their arguments placed in the introduction. If it is hidden, try to rephrase it. ex) Not all American dogs are fat.->Some American dogs are fat.

3) For narrative-carefully read the time markers for changes and figure out the hidden message (or argument) which is usually placed toward the middle to the end. Time markers represent different points in time. These are the points that mark important actions or changes in situations.

Also pay careful attention to the main character's speech and behavior and the conclusion of the story as they represent the author's ultimate message.

4) For exposition-carefully read the beginning part of each paragraph (the topic sentence) or read the part before each example. It is usually there.

5) Look for modalities or words that represent possibilities, coercion, or permission. Instead of making a strong claim, he may present a more moderate statement.

a. possibilities: can, may, might, probably,

ex) He might win the race.

b. coercion: must, have to, should, ought to, required, essential, necessary

ex) People must recycle.

c. permission: can, allow

ex) Gay marriages should be allowed in a democratic society.

6) Look for contrastive signals. Usually, the main idea comes after these contrastive signals. Also pay attention to negative words (none, no, not, never) or words that contain negative meanings in them (pejorative, derogatory, seldom). These also represent sharp turns.

7) Look for words like, "interesting," "understandable," and many others as the author finds something interesting or understandable. If he/she thinks that A is interesting, that is his/her argument.

8) Look for strong words such as "undeniable," "requires/deserves attention." "criticize" Also look for words that are <u>sharp</u> or <u>critical</u>. When we hear something important, we say, "That person has a point." Arguments are sharp edges that you don't want to miss when you read through texts. Imagine that you are a blind person reading the Braille system[1] at the tip of your fingers. When you touch a sharp edge, or the part that has a strong feel, stop and see if the part contains any important argument. <u>Do not overlook the obvious or noticeable parts in the text.</u>

---

[1] the book for the blind where a series of dots are raised (or embossed) on a piece of paper. The Braille system has its alphabets in binary dots and blind people can read texts at the tip of their fingers.

9) Sometimes the author boldly states what he/she thinks by saying, "I think…" "I argue that…" This actually does happen quite frequently.

10) If there are two passages, then, they are usually the opposites. However, they usually share a common point of view. Usually, they share the common purpose. It is their approaches/methods that differ.

Remember. Not all these signals represent the author's main argument. So, make your judgments wisely and move on.

READING
10. QUESTION TYPE-2

3. Detail Questions

Detail questions ask for specific facts not for general ideas.

1) Answer the question. Simply because an answer choice is found in the passage, it cannot always be the answer.

2) The detail question answers usually contain specific figures (10cm) or names (tarantula).

When you face questions that starts with, "According to Line 13…"

1) Most detail questions come out in order.

2) Read 2-3 sentences before/after the blank or the underlined sentence.

3) Fill in the blank with your own answer and then find the best match from the answer choices.

4. Word in the Context Questions

Word in the context questions usually start like the following:

> The word "supported" nearly means…

1) Read several lines before and after the word to connect the ideas.

2) Think if the word was used as a part of a conventional expression. ex) travel light-here "light" is not used to "illuminate."

3) Eliminate and make the best guess.

5. Similarity/Difference Questions

Similarity/difference questions start like the following.

> A is similar to B in that it…
> A differs from B in that it…

1) Think why this similarity/distinction is important to the author or to his argument.

2) Look for similarity signals (e.g. similar, resemble).

3) Look for contrast signals (e.g. but, different).

4) Read A and B and write the similarities and differences (Draw a table).

6. What is mentioned/not mentioned?

What is mentioned/not mentioned questions look like the following:

ex1) Which of the following is mentioned/not mentioned in the passage?
ex2) All of the following are true/mentioned except…

Where is the question? If the question number is 17, then the answer should be between the answers of 16 and 18 in the passage.

These are rather laborious detail type questions you would have to find one by one. Sometimes, you would have to look through the whole passage, but sometimes, you can just look at a certain section. So, act wisely.

1) Simply find what is mentioned/not mentioned. Beware that most of the answer choices are rephrased and some have traps. Also watch out for overgeneralizations/absolute statements.

ex) overgeneralization

<u>All</u> Americans are good-looking.

Let's be real. Even though many Americans are good looking, not all of them are good-looking.

ex) absolute statement

The Manchester United will <u>always</u> win the European Championship.

The Manchester United is one of the strongest soccer teams in Europe, but they cannot always win the European Championship.

2) Look for statements or sentences with simple facts and details.

3) Look for areas where a list of facts or accurate descriptions are clustered.

4) Watch out for partially incorrect contents. They are traps.

READING
11. QUESTION TYPE-3

7. Suggestion Questions

Suggestion questions start by saying, "In Line 27, the author suggests that…"

In this type, the author is making an argument. He could be suggesting the following three:

1) Prove a point.

2) Point out a problem.

3) Provide a solution.

8. Assumption Questions

Assumption questions ask us what the author had in mind at the time of writing the text. It could be his/her philosophy, a principle, or even a pet theory. It is the fundamental idea that his claim is based upon.

Assumption questions look like the following:

ex) The author makes which of the following assumptions? The first type asks for the author's conclusion.

ex) The sentence that begins with "........." depends on what assumption?

<u>premise</u>->conclusion

The assumption type questions ask us about the author's premise which logically leads to an obvious conclusion. If you have found the author's main argument, you can guess where he is coming from. Is he a Republican or a Democrat? Does he believe in global warming or not? Does this person think that recycling is necessary or not? and WHY? If you can answer this "Why?" question, you are very close to the answer.

The ETS usually asks you to take a careful look at a particular paragraph or two. Read it thoroughly and look for evidence for your guess.

Sometimes the author's argument/thought may change in the middle of the passage. A more challenging type of question would ask us, "What did the author assume in the first place?" This is a tricky question.

What had the author assumed and later didn't come true? Yes, the author had assumed that global warming would soon disappear and the ice age would come. However, with some new findings, he changed his mind. Right?

So, what is my advice? Start from the author's obvious conclusion and go back to his/her assumption. Think where the author is coming from.

9.   Inference & Implication Questions

Inference or implication questions usually start like this.

The author in the passage implies that…
What can you infer from the underlined part in the paragraph?

1) The answers for inference and implication questions are usually not in the paragraph. You need to find the clue(the most relevant information), and rephrase it.

e.g. What does the clue say?

2) Then, match with the best answer choice.

3) Always think why the author suggests the idea or why you think it is important.

READING
12. QUESTION TYPE-4

10. Author's Attitude & Tone of Voice

The author's attitude and tone of voice questions look like this.

> The author's attitude toward Z is…
> The author's tone of voice is…

1) "Suggest" means to "argue" or "mean."

2) Most passages on standardized tests come from reputable writers who seldom make irrational statements (Nobel/Pulitzer Prize winners). Sometimes they may make simple straightforward statements (A is B) but not always. Sometimes, they will make rather subtle and complicated statements. (Some are A, but some are B.).

3) For tone of voice questions,. watch out for similar words. **If there are two answer choices with similar meanings, they cannot be the answer.**

Ex) sarcasm ≒ cynicism ≒ innuendo.

According to many test developing experts, multiple choice questions have to have one best answer.

Please be prepared to know some of the most commonly appearing tones. The list can be accessed at the address below. It is called, "Tone of Voice Vocabulary List." If you access it, you will understand why you have to know a lot of SAT/GRE vocabulary.

www.likesat.com/sat

READING
13. QUESTION TYPE-5

Organization Type questions

Some of the reading questions ask students how a passage is organized. Review the 18 idea signals (Chapter 3) and 11 idea sequences (Chapter 4). Remember that most expository essays follow the general->specific pattern. Then what are some of the common patterns?

argument+example (evidence)
argument+criticism (rebuttal)
problem+solution
argument 1+counter-evidence(raises a question)+argument 2

Also, drawing an expert table (Chapter 10) will also help you understand the passage (s).

Examples

There are four example types.

1) Historical/Current events-dated, reference to the source. Most convincing.

2) Literary-from literature such as novels and poems. Used to either critique it or use it as a support.

3) Hypothetical-not dated or no reference to the source, less convincing as it suggests a situation or an incident that can happen to somebody or anybody (ex. If you were the doctor would you tell a white lie to your terminal patient?)

4) Personal-dated and reference to the source, less convincing as it can only happen to an individual or to a minority group.

Remember that in an exposition, the argument comes first and examples come later. Another point that you should remember is that writers use examples for a reason. There is no doubt that the most vivid description of a fact or an incident convinces the reader, but they don't always use historical examples. Different examples are for different occasions. That is why we have a handful of example type questions. The following a list of vocabulary that may help you distinguish the purposes of using examples in the passage.

1. reference to/point out-the author is using the example as a reference to something or the author is using the example to point at something in the passage. If there is an irony or a paradox, he/she will say it.

2. agree upon-the author is using the example/quotation because he agrees to the idea.

3. challenge/criticize/critique/refute/reject-the author is using the example to criticize a theory or an argument.

4. provide evidence-the author is using the evidence to provide evidence for his argument.

For more of these vocabulary, go to "author's tone questions in Chapter 8 and quotation questions (Question type 11) later in this Chapter.

Metaphor/Simile/Personification/Literal Expressions/Irony/Paradox

▶ Metaphor: The man=>Wolf (pick a representative characteristic).

ex) The man is a wolf.

▶ Simile: A is like B or A acts like B.

ex) The man cries like a wolf.

▶ Personification: giving human traits to other living things or to non-human objects.

ex) The clock knew my sorrow. My diary loves me and remembers me. The blanket gave me a warm hug.

▶ Literal: Human =>Selfish (pick a literal characteristic).

ex) The man is selfish.

▶ Irony: Something unexpected has come or someone says something and its opposite happens.

ex) The Ship Titanic was called, "the unsinkable," when it was constructed, but it sank on her first voyage.

▶ Paradox: a statement/situation that contradicts what it says.

ex) War is peace. Freedom is slavery. Ignorance is bliss.

Causality and Correlation

Scientific reasoning is a process of ruling out unnecessary or irrelevant variables in search of truly essential and pertinent factors. In most cases, there is no unitary causality; there are only multiple correlations.

Causality: A causes B (fact)
Correlation: A is related to B.

Validity and Reliability

Validity and Reliability are two very important concepts in any scientific investigation and if you go to college with these terms in your brain, you will be quite welcomed by professors.

▸ Validity: tests the effectiveness of your method that you are employing. Is your method (experiment) measuring what you are trying to measure?

If your cat is fat, how will you measure it? By measuring his weight or by measuring the percentage of body fat? weight in relation to height? There are so many ways to measure your cat's obesity. Moreover, there could be many other environmental factors that hinder you from doing things correctly. Are you controlling those irrelevant factors (or variables) for the accuracy of your results? These are the issues that you need to worry about and validity should be confirmed.

▸ Reliability: tests whether your method can give the same/similar results when repeated. Is it dependable and trustworthy? Is it a useful tool in finding out what you want to find out.

The SAT, GRE, and the TOEFL are considered to be fairly reliable. If you take one of these without studying them, you will get the same or similar results. Their validity and reliability are relatively high because they are tested many times before each release.

The test questions that ask about validity and reliability would look like the following:

The author would find the method/experiment in passage A as

The author sees the result of the finding (line 28) as

The answer choices would look like these:

a) valid
b) reliable
c) untrustworthy
d) irrelevant

Analogy

What is the relationship between the two concepts or two situations? This is what most analogy questions ask us. We use analogies to argue that two different situations can be seen as the same. An analogy question would like this:

ex) A hermit crab is most analogous to…

Basically, you have to build a logical relationship or a story with the given items/ideas.

1) painter : paint brush = writer : pen

Here, a painter uses a paint brush to create art just like a writer uses a pen to create a novel.

2) Getting into Harvard is as difficult as finding a needle in a haystack.

The difficulty of getting admitted to Harvard is compared to finding a needle in a haystack.

11. The Quotation Use Questions

The quotation use questions look like the following.

ex) The author used the quotation because…
The quotation primarily serves to…

1) Find the author's argument.

2) Look for words like, "in order to~," "to~" or "because" "for." These signal the reasons for the use of the quotation.

3) Authors quote famous people's sayings to borrow their authority. In other words, they use these quotations to support their arguments.

4) Authors quote famous people's sayings to present counter-arguments. If this is the reason, there has to be words like "but" or its variants.

12. The Author Criticizes A Questions

The author criticizes A questions looks like the following:

ex) The author criticizes writer A for which of the following reasons?
1) Find the author's argument.

Try to relate the main idea with the quotation (or what A says).

2) Find the argument that is opposite to it.

Look for the opposite arguments or ideas in other parts of the passage and see how the author treats it. Is he against it? Remember, the longer one write, the more one repeats himself/herself.

3) Look for words like, "in order to~," "to~," or "because" "for." These signal the reasons for the author's criticisms.

Sometimes the author explicitly states what he wants to say in the passage. However, very often these purposes are hidden. Why? Because the author thinks highly of you. He/she thinks that the reader can read and understand the hidden motive. Good writers allow his/her readers to connecting the dots.

13. Strengthen or Weaken Questions

In Strengthen/Weaken questions, you are asked to choose an factor/evidence that would strengthen/weaken the argument. In simple terms, you have to find something that would empower the author's argument.

Ex) We should build new factories in our community.

▸ Strengthen: New factories can develop the economy.

In order to add more power to the author's argument, you are to think of the most <u>compelling</u> evidence. Or something that would work best among the answer choices is also fine.

▸ Weaken-in order to weaken the author's argument, be on the opposite side of the author.

Premise-----------------------------Conclusion

In any argument, there needs to be a premise and a conclusion. You are connecting two ideas; the premise is the evidence or a reason, and the conclusion is the natural/reasonable decision/action.

In order to weaken an argument, you can do two things.

1) Prove that the premise is wrong.
2) Prove that the link (relationship) between the premise and the conclusion is weak.

Ex) We should not build new factories.
Weaken: New factories can cause more pollution.

To find the statement that is most weakening the author's argument, simply put yourself on the opposite side of the author.

Author<-------------------->Me

Author	Me
We should build new factories for economic reasons.	We should not build new factories because factories pollute the environment and it will only harm the economy in the long run.

Your reasons (the underlined part in the passage) should be compelling. Once you have found a good reason to refute the author's argument, start sifting through the answer choices and eliminate the distracters. Sometimes, you will find evidences/reasons that are similar to yours, or better ones.

READING
14. PRACTICE QUESTIONS

Practice Your Knowledge and Skills!

Having reviewed different types of reading questions, you are ready to test your knowledge and skills. On the next page are two sets of reading questions. They are a continuum of the previous narrative and expository passages. Good luck!

Reading Comprehension Question Set 3
-Narrative

The following passage is adapted from a short story written in the 19th ce ntury.

It seemed to me as though I were looking into her soul, just as I had into Monsieur Chantal's; that I was looking right fro m one end to the other of this humble life, so simple and de voted. I felt an irresistible longing to question her, to find (75)out whether she, too, had loved him; whether she also had s uffered, as he had, from this long, secret, poignant grief, whi ch one cannot see, know, or guess, but which breaks forth at night in the loneliness of the dark room.

I said to her in a low voice, like a child who is breaking a toy (80)to see what is inside: "If you could have seen Monsieur C hantal crying a while ago it would have moved you."

She started, asking: "What? He was weeping?"

"Ah, yes, he was indeed weeping!"

"Why?" She seemed deeply moved.

(85)I answered, "On your account."

"On my account?"

"Yes. He was telling me how much he had loved you in the d ays gone by; and what a pang it had given him to marry his c ousin instead of you."

(90)Her pale face seemed to grow a little longer; her calm eye s, which always remained open, suddenly closed so quickly th at they seemed shut forever. She slipped from her chair to th e floor, and slowly, gently sank down as would a fallen garme nt.

(95)I cried: "Help! help! Mademoiselle Pearl is ill."

Madame Chantal and her daughters rushed forward, and whi le they were looking for towels, water and vinegar, I grabbed my hat and ran away. I walked away with rapid strides, my he art heavy, my mind full of remorse and regret. (100)And yet s ometimes I felt pleased; I felt as though I had done a praisew orthy and necessary act. I was asking myself: "Did I do wron g or right?" They had that shut up in their hearts, just as som e people carry a bullet in a closed wound. Will they not be ha ppier now? It was too late for their (105)torture to begin ove r again and early enough for them to remember it with tende rness.

And perhaps some evening next spring, moved by a beam of moonlight falling through the branches on the grass at their f eet, they will join and press their hands in memory of all this (110)cruel and suppressed suffering; and, perhaps, also this s hort embrace may infuse in their veins a little of this thrill wh ich they would not have known without it, and will give to th ose two dead souls, brought to life in a second, the rapid and divine sensation of this intoxication, of this (115)madness w hich gives to lovers more happiness in an instant than other men can gather during a whole lifetime!

"Mademoiselle Pearl" by Guy de Maupassant (1850-1893)

10. In "It seemed…Chantal's" (line 71-72) the author means that
(A) Monsieur Chantal had been waiting for Mademoiselle Pe arl
(B) Monsieur Chantal still had feelings towards his wife.
(C) Mademoiselle Pearl and Monsieur Chantal shared the sa me feelings
(D) Mademoiselle Pearl and Madame Chantal were also cous ins
(E) Monsieur Chantal had given pain to Mademoiselle Pearl

11. The word "poignant" in line 76 means
(A) heuristic
(B) acute
(C) disproving
(D) derogatory
(E) unaffecting

12. Mademoiselle Pearl responds to the statement (line 85-86) by

(A) questioning back to the speaker about the narrator's state
ment
(B) refusing to answer the question posed to her
(C) refuting the argument posed by the narrator
(D) assessing the validity of the narrator's statement
(E) arguing her right to know what is going on

13. In line 86, "on my account" refers to
(A) the billiard game
(B) Monsieur Chantal's crying
(C) Madame Chantal's failed marriage
(D) the narrator's tale
(E) Mademoiselle Pearl's story

14. The author seems to suggest that
(A) Mademoiselle Pearl and Monsieur Chantal couldn't marr
y for a reason
(B) Mademoiselle Pearl had financial issues that hindered her
from getting married
(C) Madame Chantal had no inkling of the affair between the
two
(D) Mademoiselle Pearl had remained an old maid because o
f Madame Chantal
(E) Monsieur Chantal always practiced moral values that met
with the standards of the day

15. "She…garment," (in line 92-94) the author is using a
(A) metaphor
(B) simile
(C) personification
(D) hyperbole
(E) symbolism

16. In "I grabbed…away." (line 97-98) and in "And… please
d" (line 100), the author's action and attitude are
(A) unchanged
(B) paradoxical

(C) self-questioning
(D) assuming
(E) consistent

17. The author would most likely agree that
(A) debate on what is right or wrong is sometimes necessary
(B) opening up to discussions to create problems is necessary
(C) pressing one's memory is not good
(D) older generations need not be cruel to themselves
(E) cherishing one's deepest feelings should be kept inside

*Answers on page 190

Reading Comprehension Question Set 4
-Expository

The following passage was excerpted from a book written by a 19th Century American Author. He discusses a way of protest to the government.

Some years ago, the State met me in behalf of the Church, (95)and commanded me to pay a certain sum toward the support of a clergyman whose preaching my father attended, but never I myself. "Pay," it said, "or be locked up in the jail." I declined to pay. But, unfortunately, another man saw fit to pay it. I did not see why the schoolmaster should be (100)taxed to support the priest, and not the priest the schoolmaster: for I was not the State's schoolmaster, but I supported myself by voluntary subscription. I did not see why the lyceum should not present its tax-bill, and have the State to back its demand, as well as the Church. However, at (105)the request of the selectmen, I condescended to make some such statement as this in writing: — "Know all men by these presents, that I, Henry Thoreau, do not wish to be regarded as a member of any incorporated society which I have not joined." This I gave to the town clerk; and he has it. (110)The State, having thus learned that I did not wish to be regarded as a member of that church, has never made a like demand on me since; though it said that it must adhere to its original presumption that time. If I had known how to name them, I should then have signed off in detail from all the (115)societies which I never signed on to; but I did not know where to find a complete list.

I have paid no poll-tax for six years. I was put into a jail once on this account, for one night; and, as I stood considering the walls of solid stone, two or three feet thick, (120)the door of wood and iron, a foot thick, and the iron grating which strained the light, I could not help being struck with the foolishness of that institution which treated me as if

I were mere flesh and blood and bones, to be locked up. I wondered that it should have concluded at length that this (125)was the best use it could put me to, and had never thought to avail itself of my services in some way. I saw that, if there was a wall of stone between me and my townsmen, there was a still more difficult one to climb or break through, before they could get to be as free as I was. I did not for a (130)moment feel confined, and the walls seemed a great waste of stone and mortar. I felt as if I alone of all my townsmen had paid my tax. They plainly did not know how to treat me, but behaved like persons who are underbred. In every threat and in every compliment there was a blunder; (135)for they thought that my chief desire was to stand the other side of that stone wall. I could not but smile to see how industriously they locked the door on my meditations, which followed them out again without let or hindrance, and they were really all that was dangerous. As they could not (140)reach me, they had resolved to punish my body; just as boys, if they cannot come at some person against whom they have a spite, will abuse his dog. I saw that the State was half-witted, that it was timid as a lone woman with her silver spoons, and that it did not know its friends from its foes, (145)and I lost all my remaining respect for it, and pitied it.

Thus the State never intentionally confronts a man's sense, intellectual or moral, but only his body, his senses. It is not armed with superior wit or honesty, but with superior physical strength. I was not born to be forced. I will breathe (150)after my own fashion. Let us see who is the strongest. What force has a multitude? They only can force me who obey a higher law than I. They force me to become like themselves. I do not hear of men being forced to have this way or that by masses of men. What sort of life were that to (155)live? When I meet a government which says to me, "Your money or your life," why should I be in haste to give it my money? It may be in a great strait, and not know what to do: I cannot help that. It must help itself; do as I do. It is not worth the while to snivel about it. I am not responsible

(160) for the successful working of the machinery of society. I am not the son of the engineer. I perceive that, when an acorn and a chestnut fall side by side, the one does not remain inert to make way for the other, but both obey their own laws, and spring and grow and flourish as best they can, (165) till one, perchance, overshadows and destroys the other. If a plant cannot live according to its nature, it dies; and so a man.

From "Civil Disobedience" by Henry David Thoreau

12. Those who disagree to the author would agree to which of the following statements?
(A) Voluntary subscription is always more cost beneficial than to pay taxes.
(B) It is after all more economical to pay taxes than to live by oneself.
(C) It is much safer to pay the taxes and be protected than to live in the wilderness.
(D) The penalty can grow exponentially when one offends the government repeatedly
(E) Civil Disobedience is as grave as treason.

13. "voluntary subscription" in line 102 most nearly means
(A) bank loans
(B) government subsidies
(C) independent means
(D) mortgage payments
(E) family inheritance

14. In "Know…joined." (line 106-109) the author means that
(A) he became part of the society without his consent

(B) he should present himself in writing that he does not wish to join the State and the society.

(C) all men are regarded as members of a society through a ritual

(D) all men, including Henry Thoreau do not wish to be part of an incorporated society

(E) the State treats how the Church treats those who refuse to be a member.

15. In "account" (line 118) is most similar to
(A) history
(B) reason
(C) purpose
(D) tale
(E) report

16. In "I…up." (line 121-123) the author's tone of voice is
(A) condescending
(B) self-aggrandizing
(C) decrepit
(D) crestfallen
(E) well-accommodated

17. In line "They" refers to
(A) townsmen
(B) tax gathers
(C) prison guards
(D) neighbors
(E) the authorities

18. In line "the other side" the author means
(A) his home
(B) the prison

(C) the outside world

(D) the government

(E) the wilderness

19. "As they…dog." (line 139-142) is most analogous to

(A) a student bullying a weaker student to do his homework after realizing that he cannot do it by himself

(B) a policeman preventing the victim's family member from seeking vigilante justice after the criminal was set free

(C) a jockey looking for another horse after a lost race

(D) a professor who is treated like an outcast after his plagiarism was discovered by his colleagues

(E) a bank robber who holds a security guard a hostage as nobody else is present at the bank

20. In "It is…strength." (line 147-149) the author

(A) is praising the government's superior physical strength.

(B) finds the government armed with wit and honesty just

(C) underestimates the government and its abilities

(D) deems his own claim valid

(E) considers the government's method of tax collection reliable.

21. In "When I…money?" (line 155-157), the author suggests that

(A) one is not bound to the choices given to him/her by the State

(B) one is always obliged to make a choice when it is offered by the State

(C) one does not easily fall in a dilemma

(D) your money is the same as your life

(E) one should haste in giving his/her money to the government upon request

*Answers on page 190

READING
15. QUESTION TYPE-6

The Expert Table

Finally, the double passage questions! When you face the double passages, the Expert Table helps you understand the author's arguments, the quotations, and their relationships in double passages. This is also useful when you tackle a strengthen/weaken questions.

First, let's look at the two texts.

Text A

Animals should be kept in the zoo. Some say that zoos are waste of tax dollars. For example, Expert C reported, "Tokyo and San Francisco zoo animals did not breed and did not survive." But this was reported after a review of only two zoos, which obviously does not reflect the majority of zoos that have been quite successful at breeding and maintaining their numbers.

Text B

Are zoos really necessary? Some say that animals should be kept in zoos, but a lot of problems are involved with raising near extinct animals in captivity. Moreover, there is evidence that animals proliferate when they are left free. According to Expert D, <u>animals in the wild life preservation zones near Seoul and New York increased in population counts.</u>

Here is how you fill it out.

A's Argument	B's Argument
Expert C	Expert D

When you fill it out, it will look something like this.

A: Animals should be kept in the zoo.	B: Animals should be left in the wild.
Expert C: Tokyo and San Fr. animals did not breed and did not survive. But…	Expert D: Seoul and New York animals in the wild life preservation zones increased in pop. counts.

The double passage questions usually ask you like this.

A: Animals should be kept in the zoo.	B: Animals should be left in the wild.
Expert C: Tokyo and San Fr. animals did not breed and did not survive. But…	Expert D: Seoul and New York animals in the wild life preservation zones increased in pop. counts.

They are really all over, right? But you can do it! Let's go over them one by one.

A: Animals should be kept in the zoo.	B: Animals should be left in the wild.

The first thing you do is to find a contrasting point in between. <u>You must read both passages. Do not make any hasty judgments.</u> Usually they are in disagreement, but sometimes, B could be partially disagreeing with A. If you can't find the argument, read and re-read the examples that he/she provides. Then, go backwards and assume what the argument is.

A: Animals should be kept in the zoo.	B: Animals should be left in the wild.
Expert C: Tokyo and San Fr. animals did not breed and did not survive. But…	Expert D: Seoul and New York animals in the wild life preservation zones increased in pop. counts.

What does author A say about expert C? Why did he/she quote this? The answer is simple, right? Because there are only two choices: to use it as a support or to refute it. Do you see "But…" at the end? Yes! A quoted C to refute his argument.

A: Animals should be kept in the zoo.	B: Animals should be left in the wild.
Expert C: Tokyo and San Fr. animals did not breed and did not survive. But…	Expert D: Seoul and New York animals in the wild life preservation zones increased in pop. counts.

Now, what about B and D? Did B quote D to refute D's argument? If there is no contrastive signal like "but," then maybe D is using it to support his/her argument. Right?

A: Animals should be kept in the zoo.	B: Animals should be left in the wild.
Expert C: Tokyo and San Fr. animals did not breed and did not survive. But…	Expert D: Seoul and New York animals in the wild life preservation zones increased in pop. counts.

What would A think about what D said? He would probably disagree with D.

A: Animals should be kept in the zoo.	B: Animals should be left in the wild.
Expert C: Tokyo and San F. animals did not breed and did not survive. But…	Expert D: Seoul and New York animals in the wild life preservation zones increased in pop. counts.

How about B and C? B would probably agree to Expert C, right?

1. The Author's Arguments in two passages

This type usually looks like this:

ex) How does author A think about the argument in Passage B?

Now, with the Expert Table, you can easily answer this. Think how the selected quotation/argument can be related to Author A's argument.

2. Both passages support which generalization about C?

Here C is usually the topic. Author A and B basically want a positive change or turnout. Usually it is their methods that differ.

ex) The authors of the two passages are most similar in their…

So, let's find out their common grounds. What do these two authors agree upon? Think about that. They both agree that the animals need to be preserved and grow in population. Here, the authors differ in their choices: A finds an intervention necessary, whereas B wants no intervention.

3. Analogy Questions in the Double Passages

This type usually looks like this:

ex) What is the author's argument analogous to?

Do you remember what analogy is (See Chapter 9)? It simply means a "relationship." The most common formula is this. A is like B. Here is an example.

ex) Stealing an apple is like stealing an orange.

So, in this case, the author is saying that stealing is stealing and whether you steal an orange or an apple, both are bad. Think what the author is comparing his argument to.

Reading Exercise

Academic Genres

1. Draw a simplified version of the academic genre with explanation.

Purpose, Participants, & Context

1. What are the three things that you have to consider when you read?

2. What do you need to know for the purpose of writing?

3. What do you need to know for writer-reader relationship?

4. What do you need to know for the style (genre) of writing?

5. What are conclusion first type writings?

6. What are process first type writings?

7. Give an example of conclusion first type writing and process type writing.

Genre Distinctions

8. What two things do you have to find in a reading?

18 Idea Relation Signals

Identify 18 different idea relations and explain them in your own words.

1.

2.

3.

4.

5.

6.

7.

8.

9.

10.

11

12.

13.

14.

15.

16.

17.

18.

11 Idea Sequences

1. What are 11 idea sequences?

2. Explain linear relationship.

3. Explain deductive reasoning and provide an example.

4. Explain inductive reasoning and provide an example.

Connect the Reading Passage+Question+Answer

1. Name three ways to connect the reading passage, question, and the answer.

The Author's Idea Questions

Give four reasons why you should either mark or write the author's argument.

Main idea/Purpose Questions

What do you have to do to find the main idea or the purpose of the passage?

Narrative-

Expository

Name the remaining strategies

Detail Questions

Discuss at least 5 strategies for detail questions.

Word in the Context Questions

Name three things you need to do for this question type.

Similarity/Difference Questions

Give three strategies for similarity/difference questions.

What is mentioned/not mentioned

What do you have to watch out for in this question type?

Suggestion

Name three ways that an author makes an argument

Assumption Questions

What is the basic structure of an assumption?

What does an assumption question ask?

Inference & Implication Questions

Where is the answer for inference or implication type questions?

Author's attitude/tone of voice Question I

What are rational arguments made by famous writers? Give an example. Why is it a good argument?

From the "Attitude and Tone of Voice Vocabulary List," (can be accessed from http://www.likestudyonline.com/category/sat-tips/) select the vocabulary you do not know and create your own list.

Organization Type Questions

Name four organization patterns.

Examples

What are the four example type questions?

Analogy Questions

What is analogy? Give me an example.

Causality and Correlation

Define causality, correlation, and variable.

Validity and Reliability

Explain validity and reliability

Metaphor/Simile/Personification/Literal Expressions/Irony/Paradox

Explain metaphor, simile, personification, literal expressions, irony, and paradox, giving example of each.

Quotation Use Questions

Why does an author use quotations?

The Author Criticizes A Questions

How would you solve a "the author criticizes A questions?"

Strengthen or Weaken Questions

How would you solve strengthen or weaken questions?

The Expert Table

How would you solve a "How does author A think about the argument in Passage B?" question?

Both passages support which generalization about Z? What is a generalization?

WRITING
16. EXPOSITION

Significance, Credibility, and Sophistication

When we write a test essay, what kind of essay should we write? Probably the most logical and sophisticated looking one, right? Because such an essay would get us the highest score.

When we think of writing a test essay, we need to think of us listening people around us, such as our family, friends, politicians, teachers, neighbors, and celebrities on TV. We simply hear them talk or communicate with them on daily basis, but rarely do we think about the following questions.

Q1. Is everything that people talk about important, necessary, and meaningful? If so, in what way?

Q2. Is everything that people say credible?

Q3. Is everything that people say sophisticated and usable for my test essays?

Many students know that they shouldn't use personal stories (that are only meaningful to the writer himself/herself), fairy tales, neighbors' gossips, tabloid news stories, and irrelevant pieces of history on their test essays, but they end up doing so. Why? Simply because they have nothing else to write about.

ETS essay graders, college professors, and admissions officers look for high school students who read good books and articles from important and credible sources such as mainstream newspapers and magazines (for current events), academic journals (for historical/modern perspectives in the arts and sciences), and classic and modern literature (for philosophical thinking).

These people also want to see something extra: your ability to write good essays. What do I mean by good?

1. Significance: meaningful content and argument.
2. Credibility: trustworthy source such as
3. Sophistication: style

However, don't worry. If you have become a high school student after reading all the books that all of your previous teachers told you to do, you have enough materials with you. You simply have to connect the dots efficiently and logically and write a relevant essay to the question.

Significance: Say Something Meaningful and Important

When you make an argument, say something meaningful and important to the US and the global world. If you are a non-native speaker of English and reside in another country, what matters a lot in the local area may not be readily understood by the essay graders were educated and living in the US. Talking about an issue only important to you and your family may not be very wise. This is why I discourage my students from using personal examples (or anecdotes). They may work sometimes, but not always.

Also, try to use a clever and meaningful argument. If you are well-read and have really pondered about many literary, philosophical, historical and current issues and you may have a philosophy of your own or at least follow one of the many beliefs and thoughts. If so, that is great. However, most of us are much more impressionable (or pudding heads) than that. We don't know much or have had enough life experiences even to claim that we know something important and meaningful.

So, here is my list of some of the most important thinkers and their ideas. It is called, "essay examples." You can access it at the address below.

www.likesat.com/sat

If you are already familiar with some of these concepts, use them in your essays. They will make your essay sound smarter.

Use them to brainstorm your ideas. Look them up on the Internet. Also, the ETS and many classic and modern literature experts in each literature field (here literature doesn't simply mean the English or World Literature, but Science, Philosophy, Art, Music, Dance, and even Movies) Also the ETS provides a list of 101 books that high school students should read. If you have the time, invest your time reading them. They are worthwhile not only for your SAT /GRE preparation, but also for your life in general.

Now is your time to study, not later!

Credibility: Support Your Argument with trustworthy sources.

Whether it is from science, literature, religion, or social studies, state your sources. The more accurate, the better they are. Claims or examples that are simply "believable" are not good enough. Be explicit and eye catching. Some of the famous incidents in history are already named, and some of the most popular scientific and social science phenomena also given names. If you know them, then name them. Name the person who first came up with it.

Sophistication: Give Your Essay a Gradual Makeover

Today, there are many talk shows and many people go through makeovers. We all have witnessed numerous ordinary people turning into people with celebrity looks. I think your essay, too, can go through a makeover. If you find the appearance of your essay dull, then give it a magic touch. You, too, can do it at your home or in the library by following my simple instructions.

1. Do not use dull examples (nothing new).
2. Do not use clichés (overused expressions).
3. Do not use anything that is too obvious or known by even the most uneducated people. Many of my mediocre students used Hitler, Schweitzer, Einstein, and Edison as examples in their essays. You don't want your essay to look like a common answer that requires no quality education.

Sophistry: for Those Who Want an Instant Makeover

You have seen people change instantly in a makeover, and you know that it's a trick. Now, how do we pretend to be sophisticated when we are not? Can we do that? We all know that we cannot be knowledgeable in all areas. Believe it or not, this is the same for our essay graders. Even some of the smartest people on Earth fail to answer the essay questions. But, the funny thing is these smart people are well aware that they can't. They are even honest (at least the "honest" intellectuals) and cool about it. So, don't worry.

There is actually a credible report by a college writing professor on how his high school students made up facts/history on their SAT essays and scored high (11/12 and 12/12 points). Not all essay graders (high school English, History teachers, and college instructors) can know both history and literature very well. **Sophistry (pretending to be sophisticated) works, too**. If you are well-read, fine. But, if you aren't, make up history and pretend to know something important. Pretend to be credible. **It works because ETS focuses more on evaluating your overall writing skills, grammar, and vocabulary use, and less on the accuracy of your specific historical or literary knowledge.**

WRITING
17. ESSAY TYPES

Argumentative vs. Expository

An argumentative essay differs from an expository essay in the level of sophistication. A simple argumentative essay presents an argument and gives simple examples that everyone knows. However, if YOU write this way, people will not buy your argument. Think of some successful politicians, journalists, and writers of today and those of the past. They all present creative and thoughtful arguments supported by well-known examples that a circle of educated people (scientists, professors, doctors, and journalists and etc.) would readily recognize.

Many politicians, and journalists write simple and their speeches and writings may appeal to people's emotions, but they may not be very scientific or rational. Actually, in today's society, even politicians and journalists should be knowledgeable in science, social science, and current events along with their professional knowledge to make a lasting impression.

That is why many political, social, and economic issues of today such as illegal aliens, nationalism, and universal healthcare are seen through the lenses of science and social sciences, tested and analyzed through scientific means. Or people won't buy it. Think of how persuasive and knowledgeable Al Gore seemed when he was an active environmentalist. Though he seemed like an ordinary politician without a doctoral degree in environmental science, when he made his presentation, he seemed to have an in-depth knowledge on the topic of global warming. Other than his great oratory skills, what made him so shine? <u>His arguments, in depth knowledge and compelling evidences.</u> The same three that you need for your test essays.

Explanatory vs. Exposition

I don't know if you are familiar with the TOEFL exam. A TOEFL exam is for non-native speakers of English who try to enter an American college. Most TOEFL reading passages or your textbooks (except stories) belong to the <u>explanatory genre</u>. <u>They define, categorize and explain concepts and phenomena at a rather simple level.</u>

However, an exposition is a more academic and professional writing submitted to respected academic journals. They define, categorize, and explain concepts, but do so at a sophisticated level.

Another major difference between these two is that exposition contains an argument. Most explanatory writings don't because their whole purpose is to explain something to the reader.

▸ Explanatory: Its purpose is to explain ideas and phenomena. Definitions/explanations of new or difficult concepts are given at the beginning. <u>They usually follow logical flow, but some follows a time flow (history passages with distinct time lines).</u>

▶ Exposition: Its purpose is to make arguments (e.g. one is better than the other or one is correct/wrong). <u>Definitions/explanations</u> of new or difficult concepts are given, but not necessarily at the beginning. <u>They are used to support the author's claim.</u>

The reading passages written by scientists, social scientists, and journalists are usually expositions as they all argue about something. Some of these may have the features of a narrative genre, but they all have arguments, hidden or revealed.

Time Flow vs. Logical Flow

▶ Time Flow: The story (or what you are about to say) flows according to time.

▶ Logical Flow: General to Specific, Categorizations and Abstractions.

How will you organize your essay? You are given a prompt and a quote. The question usually asks you to write an essay on the given topic. I would say you would be much better off by using the logical flow. Because you sound much more logical. If you use the time flow, you sound like you are telling a story. You may sound more personable and down to earth, but you don't sound like an objective person who sees things from a distance as if you are not part of anything, free of personal preference and prejudice.

Remember that the essay questions ask for your opinion on a general topic that anybody can think of and freely submit their arguments to but something that involves pretty much everyone in the society. Is war sometimes necessary? Does history repeat itself? What is heroism? What is courage? The essay questions are not about my mommy and daddy, but about something that is more common to all human beings and their societies.

WRITING
18. ESSAY SCORING CRITERIA

The table on the next page shows you the things you need in your essay for a high score. Try to avoid what's on the left. Stay on the right and you will do well.

First, you need to fill up both pages. Good writers use all of their given time and space to fully develop their essays. Many studies show that good writers write a lot. Test essay is not poetry. Furthermore, when you are trying to persuade someone (the essay grader), you need to spend some time and space to explain it to him/her, right? Imagine yourself as a salesperson. What is your number one rule? Time and thought investment!

The next thing you need to worry about is your language. Your essay needs to be a formal writing. Most forms of college writings (expositions) need to be objective and formal (of course, there are exceptions). This is what the ETS expects from you. Avoid using spoken language, slang, and clichés. Simple is good in the sense that it is clear but no more, no less. Flowery and redundant is just overdoing it. What is excellent? Using abstractions, academic and neutral language is good.

Advanced Reading, Writing, and Grammar

Length	no conclusion	Less Than 1 Page	1 Page	1 & 1/2 Page	2 Pages
Language	Poor	Fair Spoken Slang Cliché	Average Simple	Good Flowery Redundant	Excellent Abstraction Academic & Neutral
Grammar	Poor	Fair	Average	Good	Excellent
Spelling & Punctuation	Poor	Fair	Average	Good	Excellent
Organization	Poor	Fair	Average Formulaic	Good	Excellent
Examples	Not-specific Irrelevant	Hypothetical	Personal	Literary	Historical Current
Creativity	Poor	Fair	Average Formulaic	Good	Excellent
Argument	Poor Absolute Claim Irrelevant	Fair	Average	Good	Excellent counter-argument
Content	Poor Off-Topic	Fair	Average	Good	Excellent
Clarity	Poor	Fair	Average	Good	Excellent
Persuasiveness	Poor	Fair	Average	Good	Excellent
Handwriting	Poor	Fair	Average	Good	Excellent

Advanced Writing Scoring Rubric

Your grammar, spelling, and punctuation should be excellent. Always give yourself three to five minutes to look over your essay for any mistakes or errors.

Now, your organization. If you know how to write a five paragraph essay, you are good to go. But, don't be too formulaic. Also, you should have good transitions as well.

In terms of examples, you want to use literary, historical, and current examples to be most persuasive. Hypothetical examples and personal examples are also okay if you have a style. Simply remember hypothetical examples and personal examples may not be very persuasive. You can't show off your knowledge either.

Your creativity is also important. This, I mean, your argument, organization, and overall writing style. You have to be unique, interesting, and sophisticated. Just don't overdo it.

When you make an argument, make sure you do not make any absolute claims or irrelevant claims. You may support one side or support both sides. Just be reasonable. If you want to use counter-arguments or counter-examples to acknowledge the limitations of your argument, that is also smart. Be fair.

The remaining three are related to the overall picture. You should not digress too much or go off-topic. Your essay should be clear and persuasive.

Lastly, your essay should be readable. Good handwriting means a lot to readers. You don't want to make your readers uncomfortable in reading your essays, right? Accommodate them a little by presenting a nicely hand-written essay. Give them a good impression.

Do not write like how I am writing this book. I am using spoken language to be more friendly.

WRITING
19. HOW TO WRITE AN EXPOSITION

In this chapter, we are going to learn some of the important features in an expository essay. They are generalization, modality, abstraction, nominalization, condensation, subordination, comparison, contrast, and categorization.

Generalization/Modality

▶ Generalization: A generalization is an argument. It is a common pattern that people find in something through experience. Are they all true? Not necessarily.

ex) American cats are fat.
All American cats are fat (or Every American cat is fat.)
Some American cats are fat and others are skinny.
American cats are overweight in general.

▶ Modality: Modality represents different strengths of an argument. It can represent ability, possibility, permission, request, suggestion, necessity, prohibition, recommendation, prediction, promise and etc.

Scholars use them often because they want to be careful when they make a claim. By weakening the strength of their arguments, they promote sales of their arguments and ultimately win more supporters.

okay) Eating burnt food causes cancer. (possibility 100%)
better) Eating burnt food <u>may</u> cause cancer. (possibility less than 100%)

No matter how many times you test a theory, there will be exceptions. In other words, few things can ever be facts. Therefore, why not tone down your argument a bit and be more accepted, right?

Modalities come in the form of modal verbs, adjectives, and adverbs, prepositional phrases, and in many other forms.

a. modal verbs: can, may, shall, will, might, must…
b. adjectives: required, important, necessary, doubtful…
c. adverbs-possibly, probably, generally, certainly,
d. prepositional phrases: in general, at most, at least…

Master different uses of modalities when you read an article, and practice applying them in your own writing as different grammar rules may apply to them[2] (See the Modality in Chapter 21).

Abstraction

▸ Abstraction: the opposite of concrete. Something that is concrete is based on physical experience and you can refer to it directly.

ex) love, philosophy, idea, success, failure, independence

[2] Modalities in the most traditional sense follows the modal verb+verb base form (e.g. "He can eat lunch," instead of "He can <u>eats</u> lunch.").

Concrete: Something tangible. These physically exist.

ex) TV, school, a dollar bill.

Using many abstractions helps your essay look good. After many same/similar incidents, a new word is coined. Words like "freedom of speech," "child labor," came about ever since we started to practice democracy, and factories hiring children as workforce. Sometimes, new words get coined after noted historical events such as "the Nuremberg Trial" and "the Red Scare." So when you want to talk about Hitler and the Nazis, also mention the Nuremberg trial. When you want to talk about how many people were treated unfairly in the US during the cold war, mention words like "censorship," "McCarthyism," and "the Red Scare."

Nominalization

▸ Nominalization: Making verbs (or other parts of speech) into nouns.

nationalize->nationalization
enrich->enrichment

[Verb->noun]
John is sad-> John's sadness

By using nominalizations, you can condense what you want to say and discuss more. In other words, you can save time and space. Moreover, you sound sophisticated.

forests losing trees->deforestation

Replacing more common verbs with more difficult ones is also a good idea.

think about->analyze
show->indicate
make it unstable->destabilize

Here is how to apply it. You start with a nominal expression to be further discussed in detail.

My child can have <u>diverse cultural experiences</u>. He/she can <u>try different kinds of food, wear different cultural clothing, and learn different cultural history</u> without traveling to the country.

The writer initially said that he would discuss various cultural experiences. So, the content that entails it should have more specific things such as food, clothing, and history that are known to be part of "culture."

Condensation

‣ Condensation: Shortening the content or compressing many ideas to provide more information within limited time and space.

[Eating good food everyday] is necessary.
->A healthy diet

John had been seriously injured and he was just released from the hospital. So, he may perform poorly at work.
->John's recent release from the hospital may lead to poor job performance.

The aforementioned two concepts (abstraction/ nominalization) are not very different from this. Abstractions and nominalizations appear as we try to stuff information for syntactic density. If words and meanings are crowded, they seem sophisticated.

Poetry uses many condensations. In less than a page, there are words loaded with many meanings (or "double entendres") and they are neatly arranged close together. Your essay, of course, needs to make sense. If you are clever, you will even play around a bit by building creative connections with these words.

One good way to apply this into your essay is to use an abstraction or a nominalization and then further explain them in detail. You can also use them to organize and categorize your ideas. Remember, <u>General to Specific</u>? That is how you are going to write, right?

Here is an example.

ex) The <u>Korean government owns the railroad system</u>. It is negatively influencing the national economy.

->Recently, <u>the nationalization of the railroad system</u> has had a negative influence on the Korean economy.
First,…
Second,…
Third,….

The writer would use nominal expressions to open up the discussion. He condensed the first part using a nominalization so that he can expand and discuss it in detail. After that he lists a number of specific negative influences.

The writer can also connect two or more ideas in a (see meaningful idea relationships in "Advanced Reading," Chapter 3 & 4) meaningful relationship.

ex) <u>The decision was stupid</u>. <u>Everyone will know about it</u> in the near future.

-><u>The stupidity of the decision</u> will be <u>revealed</u> in the near future.

Subordination

▹ Subordination: One idea is placed underneath another. The author has to connect two or more ideas in a hierarchical relationship (i.e. one highly positioned, one lowly positioned).

There are at least three ways to use subordination.

1. Explain the cause & effect and many other relationships.

ex) He is very rich. He can buy anything.
->He is *so* rich *that* he can buy anything.
premise-------------conclusion
(The premise subordinates the conclusion).

2. Use B to explain A or build a meaningful idea relationship[3]

ex) The canary that came down with the miners died. It meant that a disaster was near. The miners started to think about escape.

->The death of a canary meant that a disaster was near.
->The dead canary signaled the miners for immediate evacuation.
->The death of a canary meant an impending disaster to the miners.

3. Make value judgments.

ex) It is a gossip. He is a fool.
-> The gossip that he is a fool is not true.

---

[3]See Chapter 3 and 4 for idea relationships and Chapter 9 for scientific methods and related vocabulary.

Also use the concept of correlation, causality, validity, and reliability and show off your knowledge.

ex) Crime rate and poverty have correlation at best; poverty does not induce crime.

Comparison/Contrast/Categorization

a. Markers of comparison: compared to, similar, not so different, resemble

b. Markers of contrast: different, contrastingly, in contrast, however, although, but, nevertheless, etc.

c. Markers of classification: first, second, third, former, latter, advantages, disadvantages, belong to, etc.

Examples

Review Chapter 9 where I discuss different examples and use them to make your readers believe what you say. Like I always say, you need to use historical and literary examples.

Some students do not provide any examples in their essays. It is absolutely necessary for you to add examples to achieve high scores. So, I am going to repeat myself.

"The most vivid description of a fact or an incident convinces the reader."

So, how should you write?

➢ Use nominal expressions (abstractions), modality, categorization, subordination and other distinctive features of exposition more often.

- ➢ If your essay sounds too narrative or reads like spoken language, then change it to academic/professional language.
- ➢ Do not assume that your reader will understand your logic automatically.
- ➢ Be analytic, authoritative and specific.
- ➢ Start the paragraph with generalization and go specific.
- ➢ Use historical/literary examples over hypothetical or personal examples.
- ➢ Avoid clichés (expressions that are overused) or proverbs. But use quotations of famous people that educated people know.
- ➢ Build clear idea relationships (correlation, causality, etc.) and provide logical support.

WRITING
20. HOW TO WRITE AN EXAM ESSAY-1

The Appearance

Your exam essay should look like a four or five paragraph essay (You can always write more) with a clear introduction body and a conclusion. We suggest at least four or five paragraphs because you need to provide more than two examples and one body paragraph is not enough for that. In terms of length, make sure you fill out both pages.

Your essay represents you. Write in good handwriting and try not to make a mess on your paper. If your essay is neat and orderly, that's what you are to them as the essay graders don't know your name, gender, age, or the school you attend. They only see you on paper. They can only make assumptions.

Also remember that these days your essay, on a standardized exam, is scored holistically, meaning that the essay graders score your essay based on its overall impression. They have a score in mind as they read it and give your essay a 4 or a 5. You want to give your essay graders a favorable impression, right?

My last word of advice on this is this. Prepare enough historical and literary examples when you practice writing the essays. <u>Do not try to experiment your vocabulary and example usage at the testing center.</u> The testing center is not a nuclear testing ground. Do it on your own or with the help of a teacher. <u>Only use the examples and vocabulary that are confirmed by a knowledgeable person.</u>

Introduction

Body 1-support 1

Body 2-support 2

Body 3-support 3 or Counter-argument

Conclusion

Introduction

Body 1-compare/contrast point 1
or advantages/disadvantages

Body 2-compare/contrast point 2
or advantages/disadvantages

Body 2-compare/contrast point 3
or advantages/disadvantages

Conclusion

The Overall Structure

Paragraph one is the introduction. You may start your essay with a famous/relevant quote to the topic that educated people know. Your readers will readily recognize that you are smart (although your readers don't know everybody and every literature on the planet). Do not ramble on pointlessly by saying, "Some people said this, and others said that." Focus on presenting a clear and thoughtful argument backed up by strong supports. Don't be wishy-washy. You can enumerate your points (e.g. first, second, third) as this will help your readers to follow your essay more easily. Remember, your introduction should be a guide through your essay.

Start the second paragraph with a topic sentence. and then provide specific examples from history, literature, and current events. Provide dates and names of incidents and people. Be accurate. You can end your second paragraph by giving a preview of your third paragraph.

Start the third paragraph with a topic sentence. and then provide specific examples from history, literature, and current events. Provide dates and names of incidents and people. Be accurate. You can end your second paragraph by giving a preview of your fourth paragraph.

Start the fourth paragraph with a topic sentence. and then provide specific examples from history, literature, and current events. Provide dates and names of incidents and people. Be accurate.

In your conclusion, you can summarize what you said in your essay and make a concluding statement. If the content and the logic of your body paragraphs were rich and convincing, you would find it easy writing this part. Don't be too specific like you were in the body paragraphs. It is time to end your argument. Be general. You may end with a quote if you want to, but try not to abuse them.

Outline

1. argument
2~3. at least 2 supports 1-2 examples each

4. argument+why

1. Argument:: We can benefit from learning about the flaws of famous figures.

2. Support 1: We can learn from the achievements of famous people, and nobody is perfect ex) Achilles, Hercules, Odysse us, Hector, Alexander the Great, Princess Diana, JFK all had personal flaws.

3. Support 2: We don't make the same mistakes as the famou s people did. ex) We don't have to live miserable lives like Syl via Plath/Virginia Wolf.

4. Counter-argument: However, not all famous people's flaw s are acceptable or valuable. ex) H. Truman using the atomic bomb on Hiroshima on civilians to stop WWII is unaccepta ble. Hitler and Churchill, too, cannot be excused from the bl ame of attacking the innocent civilians.

5. Thesis: Important lessons can be learned from the flaws of famous people without risking our lives or precious resource s. (argument+why).

WRITING
21. HOW TO WRITE AN EXAM ESSAY-2

Introduction

There are myriad ways to write an essay, but here I suggest two. Try to imitate these until you develop your own style. Sample 1 ends with a thoughtful argument, and Sample 2 ends with a preview of the body. Try not to go too specific and try not to use examples in the introduction.

Sample Introduction 1

Intro-The discovery that someone we admire has done something wrong is always disappointing and disillusioning. Yet even when people we consider heroes have been tarnished by their faults, they are no less valuable than people who appear perfect. <u>When we learn that an admired person, even one who is seemingly perfect, has behaved in less than admirable ways, we discover a complex truth: great ideas and great deeds come from imperfect people like ourselves.</u>

Sample Introduction 2

Intro-Changing decisions when circumstances change is often better than sticking to the original plan. Living in huma n society, people are often expected to stick to their original plans and be consistent. <u>However, one needs to be flexible in order to wisely adapt to fast changing situations.</u> Examples c an be given in the cases of Ralph Waldo Emerson, Bertrand Russell, and Vladimir Lenin.

Body-Emerson in his _____ essay argued that o ne does not need to be consistent.

Body

1. Try to use as many abstractions and nominalizations (big words) as possible. Try to hit the nail at once with that one word instead of beating around the bushes.

(an equal opportunity policy that allows a certain percentage of colored students to be admitted to schools that serves public: <u>affirmative action</u>) (sentencing someone to death: <u>capital punishment</u>) (right to vote: <u>suffrage</u>) (protesting without violent behavior: <u>non-violent passive resistance</u>) (human beings are free from destiny or God's plans: <u>free will</u>) (depending on each other: <u>interdependence</u>)

2. Avoid overused expressions. Substitute simple words with difficult ones.

(many->plethora)   (attend->matriculate)   (cry->lament) (cause->induce) (ignore->disdain) (to do list->agenda) (change->enhance or redirect) (honorable->dignified) (instead of->as an alternative to) (end->pull out of) (think of->devise)

3. Use nominalizations instead of simple verbs.

(prefer->preference) (disturb->deter->deterrence) (meet->engage->engagement) (use->employ->employment)

Also Search for "Action Verb List" on the Internet and replace simple verbs into action verbs as they sound more direct and sophisticated.

4. Use educated expressions, examples, and quotations from few famous people that are applicable in many different situations and practice using them.

(Descartes' "cogito ergo sum": I think, therefore I exist) (a priori: before) (magnum opus: a masterpiece) (mens rea: guilty mind) (albeit: in spite of) (tabula rasa: an empty table)

5. Try to connect your body paragraphs. Build good transitions so that your ideas flow from one to another more smoothly. The following is an example.

Sample Body

One of the most detrimental effects of technology is how it makes war more violent and destructive. For example, one of the reasons why World War I was one of the deadliest conflicts of all time is because we were able to manufacture many fatal weapons by utilizing improved technology. During this war, combatants expanded the use of catastrophic armaments, such as machine guns, combat planes and tanks. These deadly machines were made possible by the application of scientific knowledge developed by scientists, including a Dutch chemist, Fritz Haber. He used his knowledge to introduce chlorine gas, earning him the "father of chemical warfare" title.

In addition, violence can be generated by exposure to diverse media, such as television and the internet, which are also products of technology. Media Awareness Network (2010) argues that naive young people can be harmed by identifying themselves with brutality displayed in the media. This demonstrates that technology not only affects the global village, but may also increase aggression in people.

The author starts with a clear topic sentence (one of the most…) at the beginning of the body paragraph. The specific names mentioned (World War I, Fritz Haber, "father of chemical warfare," Media Awareness Network (2010)) gives power and authority to the essay. Nominal expressions were used to add syntactic density (e.g. "the application of scientific knowledge").

Also note that the transition (In addition…) between body paragraphs is smooth as the second paragraph can use the first paragraph as a base to further discuss the topic. <u>Use proper quotations or at least make your essay sound like you are quoting an important person or media.</u>

Conclusion

Rephrase and summarize in your conclusion. You can reopen your conclusion with a general statement. Then summarize your specific points that you discussed in the body paragraphs. Make a concluding statement which readily incorporates all your ideas. Do not give examples or discuss anything specifically. Do not talk about any arguments, supports, or examples that you did not mention in the body paragraphs. Be concise and stay focused.

Sample Conclusion

While we enjoy the convenience and advancements made possible by the development of technology, we must not overlook the side effects of the process. In order to assure our future existence and to prevent cataclysmal events, governments around the globe must devise plans to cope with problems facing mankind. <u>Perhaps the most</u>

crucial task humankind has to implement is to ex-cogitate an eclectic solution that will allow us to reap the benefits of technology, while not being overwhelmed by its negative aspects.

More essay samples are available in my other book, "60 Model Essays."

Writing Exercises

Significance, Credibility, and Sophistication

What three things do you need to consider in writing a test essay. Explain them.

Argumentative vs. Expository vs. Exposition

Explain each type of writing.

Time Flow and Logical Flow

Explain time flow and logical flow in your own words.

What is time flow?

What is logical flow?

		Less Than 1 Page	1 Page	1 & 1/2 Page	2 Pages
	Poor		Average Simple		Excellent
	Poor	Fair	Average	Good	Excellent
	Poor	Fair	Average	Good	Excellent
	Poor	Fair	Average	Good	Excellent
Creativity	Poor	Fair	Average	Good	Excellent
	Poor	Fair	Average	Good	Excellent
	Poor	Fair	Average	Good	Excellent
	Poor	Fair	Average	Good	Excellent
	Poor	Fair	Average	Good	Excellent
Handwriting	Poor	Fair	Average	Good	Excellent

Advanced Writing Scoring Rubric

Complete the Scoring Rubric.

Generalization/Modality

Define generalization and modality.

Abstraction

Distinguish abstract words and concrete words using your own examples.

Nominalization

What is nominalization? Give two examples.

Condensation

What is condensation? Give one example.

Subordination

Explain three ways to use subordination.

Comparison/Contrast/Categorization

Give examples of each.

Correlation

Explain Correlation. Provide an example.

Causality

Explain Causality. Provide an example.

How would you write an exposition from now on? Write a paragraph about how you would write in the future including the eight points mentioned.

_____

_____

_____

_____

_____

_____

_____

_____

_____

_____

_____

_____

_____

_____

_____

_____

_____

_____

_____

_____

_____

_____

_____

_____

GRAMMAR
22. WHAT IS GRAMMAR?

Language

▸ What is language? Language is a tool used to describe, explain or argue about social or scientific phenomena.

Grammar

What is grammar? It is a set of language rules or patterns commonly recognized and used for effective communication.

Why do language users need to know grammar? Most language users use the conventionalized linguistic patterns (i.e. it is a series of promises) because they can understand, use, and even predict things better.

Depending on the situation, an adjective can function as an adverb when an adjective can function as a noun.

▸ 1. He runs <u>fast</u>. adverb
▸ 2. He is a <u>fast</u> runner. adjective

▶ 3. There is <u>enough</u> cold water. adjective

▶ 4. The water is cold <u>enough</u> to drink. adverb

▶ 5. He has an <u>alternative</u> solution. adjective/noun

▶ 6. He has an <u>alternative</u>. noun

After all, grammar is a functional explanation of language rules/conventions. <u>It is used to name places, objects, and people or to put concepts in logical order.</u>

GRAMMAR
23. THE PARTS OF SPEECH

Parts of Speech: the Functional Elements

▸ Noun: name
▸ Verb: motion, change
▸ Adjective: state
▸ Adverb: degree, frequency
▸ Preposition: direction

Noun

▸ **Purpose:** to express/explain people, objects, particles, places, abstraction (concepts), and their groups. <u>This is why names exist.</u>
1. subject: usually the person/thing that takes the action.
2. object: usually the person/thing that is being moved or changed by someone/something else.
3. complement: the explanation of the subject.

▸ **Use:**
1. subject: <u>John</u> swims.

2. object: I like <u>ice cream</u>.
3. complement: John is <u>a teacher</u>.

▶ **Form:** -ment, -tion, -sion, -sy, <u>-ty</u>, <u>-al</u>, <u>-ive</u>, -ing, -or, -er (the underlined could also be adj.)

Verb

▶ **Purpose:**
1. verb(predicate): to describe a motion and to explain the action of the agent (or "the doer")
2. adjective(modifier): to modify(explain the state of) the following noun.

▶ **Use:**
1. verb(predicate): John <u>sings</u>.
2. adjective(modifier):
   -present participle: the <u>singing</u> John
   -past participle: the <u>drunken</u> John

▶ **Form:**
   watch out for regular/irregular present, past, past participle forms. ex) eat-ate-eaten

Adjective

▶ **Purpose:**
1. verb (predicate): to describe a state (or condition) be+adjective (e.g. I am sad.)
-be verb (copula) or become, look, seem...
2. adjective (modifier): to explain the state or condition of the following noun.

▶ **Use:**
1. verb (predicate): John is <u>sad</u>.
2. adjective (modifier): the <u>sad</u> John
-usually placed in the order of

① article+adverb+adjective+noun

or sometimes,

② adverb+adjective+article+noun

▸ **Form:** <u>-ty</u>, <u>-al</u>, <u>-ive</u>, -ly (noun+ly=adjective)

▸ **Adjective Cluster:** -<u>adjectives may appear in clusters</u>

-predeterminer+determiner+rank+number+size+general+noun

ex) Both these first two large English flowers

▸ **The placing order of general adjectives**
-personality/characteristic+size+shape+old/new+color+origin+material

ex) the first three large old blue Chinese porcelain vases

Adverb

▸ **Purpose:**
1. to modify(explains the state of) a sentence, noun, verb, adjective or adverb. (An adverb rarely modifies a noun directly).
2. to explain/describe the degree, frequency, location, and time.

▸ **Use:**
1. frequency adverb (sometimes) vs. time adverb (early, late)
2. order: frequency adverb+verb+time adverb.

ex) John <u>always</u> comes home <u>late</u>.

▸ **Form:** -ly (adjective+ly=adverb). Some adjectives can be used as adverb without adding –ly. (John eats <u>fast</u>.)

Preposition

▸ **Purpose:**
1. to indicate the direction, time or location.

▸ **Use:**
1. A preposition comes before a noun or a noun phrase. A phrase that begins with a preposition is a "prepositional phrase." A prepositional phrase cannot be the subject.
2. A preposition that follows a verb to form a verb phrase (or phrasal verb) is an adverb.

ex) put up with, deal with…

▸ **Form:** to, for, on, in, at, over….

Visit, Download & Study

▸ Many questions on grammar are on prepositions, phrasal verbs, articles, infinitives, and gerunds. Instead of going through them one by one, I suggest the following links and materials. Some are even free.

▸ Basic Lecture on Prepositions (Free)

   http://www.elihinkel.org/tips/prepositions.htm

▸ English Prepositions List (Free)

   http://www.esldepot.com/english-prepositions-list.php

▸ 1000 Phrasal Verbs in Context ($)

   http://www.teflgames.com/phrasal_verbs.html

▸ a, an, the

http://owl.english.purdue.edu/owl/resource/540/01/

▶ infinitive vs. gerunds

http://www.sonnerct.com/English_Rules/LR10_Gerun ds_Infinitives.htm

▶ Basic Grammar Practice Questions ($)

Power 3000 TOEFL Test CDROM Grammar Review: A Tutorial With 3000 Questions (150 Practice Tests) [CD-ROM]

GRAMMAR
19. FIVE SENTENCE STRUCTURES

Five Sentence Structures

There are five basic sentence structures in English.

1. S+V
   ex) John lives.

2. S+V+C
   ex) John is sad.

3. S+V+O
   ex) John likes Mary.

4. S+V+DO+IO
   ex) John gives a book to Mary. John gives Mary a book.

5. S+V+O+OC
   ex) People elected John President.

1. **S+V:**
   In this structure, the verb explains what the subject (usually the agent) does.

ex) John lives.
John eats.

John goes to school.
-> *Here, "to school" represents the direction.

2. **S+V:**
   In this structure, the verb explains what the subject (usually the agent) does.

ex) John lives.
John eats.
John goes to school.-> *Here, "to school" represents the direction.

3. **S+V+O:**
   This structure explains what one (Subject/agent) does to an object (person/object/environment).

ex) John likes Mary.
John eats vegetable.

4. **S+V+DO+IO:**
   This structure explains what the subject does to an object (DO) to a recipient (IO).

ex) John gives <u>Mary</u> <u>a book</u>.
           IO   DO
John gives <u>a book</u> <u>to Mary.</u>
          DO   IO

5. **S+V+O+OC:**
   The subject(S) is usually chosen or selected to be given or placed in a position (O). So, the object (O) represents the position and the object complement (OC) explains the object.

ex) People elected <u>John</u> <u>President</u>.
                    O   OC

GRAMMAR
25. QUESTION TYPE-1

Connectionism

If you are pondering over two or three answer choices, then, connect the question and answer and see which one makes most sense.

For example, if answer choice (a) and (b) are attractive to you, then write as the following:

(a) Q)----------------------------Ans)-----------------------
(b) Q)----------------------------Ans)-----------------------

Doing this will help you see the distinctions more clearly.

Relative Pronouns/Adverbs

▶ Relative Pronoun: is used to avoid repeating the same noun which comes in the subject, object, and adjective positions

▸ Relative Adverb: is used to avoid repeating the same noun which comes in the adverb position. Here, adverbs are used to represent time and location, not to modify other parts of speech or a sentence.

▸ **which**: referring to a group, object or animal. when you can choose one among many. When "which" follows a preposition (e.g. in which), "that" cannot be used. (i.e. there is a "choice.")

▸ **that**: referring to a group, object or person. It can be used as a subordinating conjunction or as relative pronoun. It is almost substitutable with "which." However, when used to represent "the best" or "the only" "the very first", that must be used.

▸ **what**: referring to a thing or object that cannot be chosen among many. (i.e. there isn't necessarily a "choice."

▸ **who**: referring to a person or animal in the subject position.

▸ **when**: referring to a specific time.

▸ **where**: referring to a place. Substitutable with in/on/at which

▸ **whom**: referring to a person in the object position.

▸ **whose**: referring to a person/object in the object position (the possessive of who/which is whose.).

▸ **on which, at which, to which, by which=where.** Referring to a specific location.

ex) The book was placed <u>on which</u> I sat down.

▸ **what for=why.** Referring to a specific reason.

▶ **antecedent+relative pronoun (that, which)=what.**

ex) <u>The book that</u> I want-> <u>what</u> I want is…

Subject-Verb Conjugation

Subject-Verb Conjugation: means that the subject and the verb need to match in number.

ex) <u>John likes</u> his coat.
<u>Everybody has</u> his duty.

Since almost everyone is aware of this, we will go into the following question types which appear on the test frequently.

Insertion

Insertions questions are easily identifiable as they contain two commas. If they are making it difficult from identifying the error quickly, just put them in parentheses.

▶ Phrase Insertion (word apposition)

X-Mercury (, one of the planets,) <u>it</u> is closer to the sun than the Earth.

Here, the sentence is incorrect as both "Mercury" and "it" are subjects and "it" needs to be crossed out.

▶ Sentence Insertion (embedded sentence)

X-One of the books (that are as old as 20 years) <u>were</u> just returned to me.

The first thing to note in the sentence above is that a sentence is embedded without commas. The subject is "One," so the verb "were" should be "was." match.

X-The place, <u>that I have visited many times</u>, is not far from here.

Also remember that "that" cannot be used directly after a comma. In other words, "which" is the answer for such a question[4].

Parallelism

▸ Two or more phrases and sentences connected with coordinating conjunctions (e.g. and, but, yet, etc., See Chapter 23) should be parallel (or be equal in form, case, and status).

▸ adjective, adjective, and adjective

X- He is smart, funny, and <u>popularity</u>.
O-He is smart, funny, and popular.

▸ verb, verb, and verb

X- I eat, danced, and sleeping.
O-I ate, danced, and slept.

As you can imagine, there are also these rules:

▸ infinitive, infinitive, and infinitive
▸ gerund, gerund, and gerund
▸ noun, noun, and noun
▸ passive, passive, and passive

[4] Of course, there are always exceptions to this rule, but they usually don't appear on the SAT.

▸ phrase, phrase, and phrase
▸ sentence, sentence, and sentence

Either~ Or~/ Neither~ Nor~

▸ Either A or B and Neither A nor B +Verb
the verb that follows this structure always conjugates with B.

ex) Either John or his friends are rich.

▸ Modifier+Either A or B and Neither A nor B
the pre-modifier can modify together before either (neither)
or modify each.

ex) It is **in** either Jim's back or Janie's.
ex) It is either **in** Jim's back or **in** Janie's

A Number of vs. The Number of

1. A number of: means "many," so it is followed by a plural
   verb form.

ex) A number of students <u>were</u> happy.

2. The number of: means "the number," so it is followed by
   a singular verb form.

ex) The number of students <u>was</u> 20 in total.

GRAMMAR
26. QUESTION TYPE-2

Tenses

English tense is very complicated and I suggest you review Eli Hinkel's tenses. The website does an excellent job of explaining the different tenses and the subjunctives.

http://www.elihinkel.org/tips/tenses.htm

Simple Past vs. Present Perfect

Use the simple past tense when there is a specific date.

X-My father has passed away in 1991.

O-My father passed away in 1991.

However, use the present perfect tense to refer to duration.

Present Perfect: Since+S+have (has)+past participle

ex) Since I have finished my homework, I will go out and play.

Passive Voice and Participial Phrase

When a sentence is written in the passive voice, the agent usually should be specified.

X-John was hit by <u>it</u>.
O-John was hit by <u>a car</u>.

When the subject of a sentence is inanimate (cannot move by itself), the agent has to be specified.

X-Vacuum cleaners operate <u>when pressing a button</u>.
O-Vacuum cleaners operate <u>when a button is pressed</u>.

Simple Present vs. Present Progressive

Many people think that they should use the simple present tense to describe what is happening now, but it is actually the job of the present progressive.

▶ Simple Present: use this to describe a habit, generalization, or what is held to be true.

-Habit-I walk to school.
-Generalization(Argument)-Koreans enjoy spicy food.
-Truth-The earth is round.

▶ Present Progressive: use this to express what is happening at this moment.

ex) The volcano is exploding.

The Future Tense

The future tense is used to represent the possibility of a future event. When conditionals are used, the present tense replaces the future tense.

X-If I will go to school tomorrow, I will meet my friends.
O-If I go to school tomorrow, I will meet my friends.

Modality

▶ Modality: Modality requires the entailing verb to be in the base form. In other words, no tense or no third person singular forms on the verb. Modality takes them all.

ex) I can ate->I could eat
ex) He eats->He can eat.

Most people know up to here. But how about this?

ex) It is <u>required</u> that he <u>do</u> his homework.
    <u>essential</u>
    <u>important</u>

Here, "do" takes the base form because of the preceding modality (required, essential, important, etc.)

GRAMMAR
27. QUESTION TYPE-3

Subject Verb Inversion

When the sentence starts with "there is~" structure, the verb should be conjugated with the noun that comes after.

ex) There are <u>many cows</u>.

When the sentence starts with an adverbial(or prepositional phrase) that represents time or location.

ex) <u>In the house</u> was the thief.
    There

When the sentence starts with a strong negative word (never, seldom, hardly, rarely, etc.), the subject and the verb should be inverted.

ex) Rarely did he do his homework.

▶ Not only +V+S, but also S+V.

ex) Not only was he handsome, but also he was rich.

While vs. During

▶ While: can be followed by a clause or a phrase.

ex) While I was cooking->While cooking

Here, "I was" was omitted.

▶ During: can only be followed by a phrase.

ex) During the winter break

Before vs. Ago

▶ Before: could be any time in the past. It is usually used without a specific reference of time.

ex) I met him before.
cf.) 5 years before that

▶ ago: usually has a specific reference of time.

ex) I met him five years ago.
cf.) Long ago

Later vs. After

▶ later: could be any time in the future. It is usually used without a specific reference of time.

ex) I will see you later.

▶ after: usually has a specific reference of time.

ex) I will see you after five minutes.

Toward vs. Towards

▶ toward and towards are basically the same.

in, within, after

▶ in: when used to refer to "time", it really means "after."

ex) I will pay you back in two days.

Here, the borrower will return the money after two days.

▶ within: when used to refer to "time", it really means "between."

ex) I will pay you back within two days.

Here, the borrower will return the money before the third day.

Because, Because of, Due to

▶ Because: can be followed by a clause.

ex) Mary is jealous because John is rich.

▶ Because of: can be followed by a phrase.

ex) Mary is jealous because of John's wealth.

▶ Due to: can only be followed by a phrase and should not be used in the beginning of a sentence.

ex) Mary is jealous due to John's wealth.

Farther vs. Further

▸ Farther: Going the physical distance

ex) Let's go farther.

▸ Further: Going the (abstract/mental) depth

ex) Let's study further.

Little, Less, Lesser

▸ Little is the positive degree

▸ Less is the comparative degree of "Little." It is used to represent a smaller quantity.

ex) Generic brands are less expensive.

▸ Lesser is also the comparative degree of "Little." However, it is used to represent quality. It means "less important," or "less valuable."

ex) the lesser nations

Economic vs. Economical
Historic vs. Historical

▸ economic-related to economy
▸ economical-cheap

▸ historic-has importance
▸ historical-is simply recorded in history may not be very important.

GRAMMAR
28. QUESTION TYPE-4

Subjunctive

The subjunctive can be used when the present situation is the opposite of reality.

Ex) X-I wish I was a bird.
    O- I wish I were a bird.

Meaning: I am not a bird right now, but I wish I were one.

ex) I wish I were rich.

Meaning: I am not rich right now, but I wish I were rich.

Subjunctive: Present Unreal

The subjunctive mood can be used when the present situation is the opposite of reality.

▶ Subjunctive Present Unreal: the opposite of the present condition

Formula:

> If+S+past tense verb, S+would+verb…
> could
> might

ex) If I were a bird, I could fly to you.

Meaning: I am not a bird right now, but I wish I were one.

Subjunctive: Past Unreal

▶ Subjunctive Past Unreal: the opposite of the past condition

Formula:
If+S+had+past participle, S+would+have+past participle.

ex)If I had been a bird, I could have flied to you.

Meaning: I was not a bird in the past, therefore, I could not fly to you.

Subjunctive: Mixed Subjunctive

The action in the past influences the present.

If+S+had+past participle, S+would+verb

ex) If I had saved money 20 years ago, I would be rich now.

Subjunctive+SV Inversion

If I were a bird
If I had been a bird

The subjunctive clauses above can be made more concise and inverted in the following way.

If I were a bird->Were I bird
If I had been a bird->Had I been a bird

I Wish, As If

Remember that "I wish," and "as if" are also subjunctives.

I wish I <u>was</u> a bird.
->I wish I <u>were</u> a bird

He talks as if he <u>was</u> an American.
->He talks as if he <u>were</u> an American.

29. ABOVE SENTENCE LEVEL GRAMMAR

So far, we have dealt with sentence level grammar. From now on, we will discuss sentential relationships and above. There are fewer rules in sentential relationships, so don't worry. You simply have to understand things. That is why, from this point on, we focus less on grammaticality, but more on clarity and conciseness.

Phrase and Clause

▶ Phrase: meaningful chunks that do not have both subject and verb. If it only has one of the two, then it is a phrase. However, if it has both(S+V), then it is a clause.

ex) In the house, after lunch, at school

▶ Clause: a meaningful chunk that has both subject(S) and verb(V).

ex) I eat, John has a book, Mary is happy.

Phrase + Clause

How many connecting devices do you need when you connect phrases and clauses?

▸ phrase+phrase: You don't need a connecting device (conjunction, relative pronoun/adverb, colon or semi-colon) between phrases,

ex) in the morning/at five.

although you could use "and" or "but." to put two phrases of equal status.

ex) in the morning **and** in the afternoon

▸ phrase+clause: You don't need a connecting device.

ex) In the morning,/ I eat breakfast.

▸ clause+phrase: You don't need a connecting device.

ex) I run /at the gym.

▸ clause+clause

You need one connecting device (conjunction, relative pronoun/adverb, colon (:) or semi-colon (;)).

▸ clause+clause+clause

You need two connecting devices (conjunction, relative pronoun/adverb, colon (:) or semi-colon (;)) for three sentences and three for four sentences.

Run-on Sentence

If there is no conjunction, relative pronoun/adverb, colon (:) or semi-colon (;) between clauses, it is called a "run-on sentence."

ex) *I am sick I go home.<---a run on sentence.

Rarely can two sentences be combined without a conjunction, relative pronoun/adverb, colon or semi-colon.

Conjunction, Relative Pronoun/Adverb

Conjunctions and relative pronouns/adverbs are used to connect clauses. Between two sentences, there should be one conjunction or one relative pronoun. Among three, there should be two.

▶ -Coordinating Conjunctions: comes in between two similar/equal status.

ex) and, but, or, nor, yet, so

▶ -Subordinating Conjunctions: only happens when a condition is satisfied.

after	as	now that
till/until/'til	as if	provided (that)
although	as though	wherever
even if	as long as	since
even though	as much as	while
if	as soon as	because
unless	inasmuch	that
lest	in order that	so that

before	so that	where if
even	supposing	whereas
in order that	than	wherever
just as	how	whenever
now	no matter	whatever
once	while	whoever
rather than	whether	whichever

▸ Relative pronouns and relative adverbs are part of subordinating conjunctions.

▸ Relative Pronouns: represents a noun in the subject, object, or complement position.

ex) which, what, who, whom, that…

▸ Relative Adverbs: represents time, place, and reason

ex) where, why, when

:(Colon) and ;(Semi-colon)

Like conjunctions and relative pronouns (adverbs), colon and semi-colon can be used to connect two clauses (or sentences). Usually both colon and semi-colon comes after a clause.

▸ Colon: use colon to list phrases (ex: noun phrases) or connect two sentences.

ex) There are only two types of people on earth: Beatles lovers and Elvis lovers.

ex) I have two pretty coats: one is pink, and the other is yellow.

▶ Semi-colon: use semi colon to connect two sentences (conjunctive adverbs: however, therefore, in addition, moreover, subsequently, consequently, instead and additionally).

ex) Michael's family runs a casino; however, Andy is a musician.

ex) Don's family runs a meat packing business; therefore, Andy can't be a musician.

▶ Semi-colon: use semi colon to give examples or a list (for instance/for example). A semi-colon has the meaning of "and" or "but."

ex) The Corleone runs many businesses; for example, restaurant, oil, hotel, and theater.

▶ Semi-colon: use semi colon to give examples or a list.

ex) Last summer, I visited many cities: Los Angeles, California; Denver, Colorado; and Salt Lake City, Utah.

ADVANCED GRAMMAR
30. QUESTION TYPES

So far, we have dealt with sentence level grammar. From now on, we will discuss sentential relationships and above.

Subject vs. Agent

You need to distinguish a subject from an agent. If you don't, you will be easily deceived by the distracters. They would all look the same to you. Especially, you can easily miss the modifier/modified questions.

▸ Subject: usually the first noun that is related to the action (motion) of the sentence. It can be the "doer" or the "object of action."

ex) <u>John</u> built the house.

Here the subject is "John."

ex) <u>The house</u> is built by John.

Here the subject is "The house."

▶ Agent: the actual doer. An agent makes things happen.

ex) <u>John</u> built the house.

Here the agent is "John."

ex) The house is built by <u>John</u>.

Here the agent is still <u>John</u>, because he made things happen.

Modifier/Modified

▶ Modifier (word, phrase or clause): A modifier explains what is being followed. It usually comes before the modifier, but sometimes it can come after the modified word.

ex) <u>Happy</u> John

▶ Modified (word, phrase or clause): A modified is the word that is being explained. It usually comes after the modifier.

ex) Happy <u>John</u>

▶ Pre-modifier: comes before the word that is being modified.

ex) <u>Happy</u> John

▶ Post-modifier: comes after the word that is being modified.

ex) Surgeon <u>General,</u> Something <u>Special</u>

The book <u>that is on sale</u> is very popular.

▶ The modifier and the modified should be placed right next to each other or it can cause confusion.

X-While taking the test, <u>the pencil</u> was broken.

Here, the pencil was not taking the test, so it should be re-written as the following.

O-While taking the test, <u>the student</u> broke the pencil.

Also, some grammar questions have misplaced modifiers and modifieds.

ex) Mr. Kim from Canada ate the candy.

meaning) Mr. Kim who is from Canada ate the candy.

ex) Mr. Kim ate the candy from Canada.

meaning) The candy is from Canada.

ETS tries to fool you like this. So, try to figure out what the author is trying to say and then choose the closest answer.

Direct Object vs. Indirect Object

Knowing this distinction also helps you understand what to do with passive sentence questions and subject-verb inversion questions.

▶ Direct Object: the object that is actually being moved.

ex) John gave Mary <u>the book</u>.

‣ Indirect Object: the direction, destination or the person the object is being moved to.

ex) John gave <u>Mary</u> the book.
   John sold the book <u>to the bookstore.</u>

‣ Any word that starts with a preposition cannot be the subject of the sentence (Subject Verb Inversion).

ex) <u>In the house</u> was John.

   Here, the subject is not "the house," but it was John.

31. CLARITY AND CONCISENESS

Clarity and Conciseness are two very important concepts in the grammar section. Let's discuss them in detail.

Clarity (Reference)

▸ Clarity: The writer/speaker should be explicit about what he/she is discussing. There shouldn't be ambiguity or too many abstractions.

1. Who is the doer?
2. What is he doing to what/whom?

ex) The garbage was dumped. (by who?)

▸ If a sentence/paragraph gets too long with many subjects and verbs, then there are too many agents to choose from. In this case, the agents and the referents should match or the reader/listener will be confused.

ambiguous) Many teachers and students were present at the conference, however, <u>they</u> were not presenters.

Here, "they" is ambiguous; it could be teachers or students.

clear) Many teachers and students were present at the conference, however, the students were not presenters.

Conciseness

▶ Conciseness: The writer/speaker should not discuss the matter for too long. There shouldn't be too many details or modifications.

redundant) He became smart and intelligent.

Here, "smart" and "intelligent" are the same thing.

Concise) He became smart.

▶ Flowery Sentences: The writer/speaker should not use too many modifications to embellish the sentence.

flowery) The glimmering, golden rays of the brilliant orb of the sun shimmered above the white-hot sands of the vast desert, sere and lifeless.

improved) The rays of the sun shimmered above the hot, dry desert.

Here is a trick. If you don't know what to choose from in a grammar question, simply choosing the shortest sentence among the answer choices could be your educated guess. Modern English users prefers word economy.

GRAMMAR
32. S.M.A.R.T.

In order to miss fewer questions on the grammar section, you need a mental framework that allows you to sift through the distracters. You simply write down S. M. A. R. T. and write down everything that comes to your mind.

▶ S-Subject Verb Conjugation/S-V Inversion/Subjunctive /Strong Negation

-Ask: Where is the subject? Where is the verb? Do the subject and verb match in number and gender? Are the subject and verb inverted? Is it subjunctive? Does the sentence start with a strong negative word such as rarely, never, seldom? If so, then there can be no double negatives, and the subject and the verb should be inverted (ex: Seldom does he eat.../Never has he eaten a Mango...)

▶ M-Modifier/Modified/Modality

-Ask: Are modifier and modified placed next to each other? Is there a modal verb(may, can, must)?

▶ A-Article(a, an, the)/Adverb/Agent/Ambiguity(Clarity)

-Ask: Is the article used correctly? Is the following noun countable or non-countable? Regardless of the subject in the sentence, who is the agent("the actual doer") Who is taking the action? Who are referred to as "they"? Is the author referring to John or Mark in the sentence when he says he? (ex: John gave Mark <u>his</u> jacket.). Is "you" and "one" used together to refer to the same person? The author has to be consistent with its usage.

▶ R-Parallelism/Preposition/Phrasal Verb
  /Run-on Sentence/Relative Pronouns (Adverbs)/

-Ask: Are the words listed in similar forms (I like to eat, drink, and swimming)? Is the preposition or adverb used correctly? Is the phrasal verb used correctly? Is it a run-on sentence? Two clauses should be connected with a conjunction, relative pronoun, colon, or a semi-colon.

▶ T-Verb Tense

-Ask: Do the verb tenses match? Are they consistent?

Grammar Exercise

Grammar

What is language?

What is grammar?

Noun

Explain the purpose, use, and form.

Verb

Explain the purpose, use, and form.

Adjective

Explain the purpose, use, and form.

Adverb

Explain the purpose, use, and form.

Preposition

Explain the purpose, use, and form.

5 Sentence Structures

What are five sentences structures? Provide one example for each.

Relative Pronouns/Adverbs

How is relative pronoun different from relative adverb?

What is relative pronoun used for?

Explain the eight relative pronouns

Name two Subject-Verb Conjugation question types we need to watch out for, and explain them.

Explain parallelism.

Explain how we should conjugate either~or~/neither~nor~

Distinguish "a number of" from "the number of"

Tenses

Distinguish the simple past from the present perfect.

Give each an example of a misuse of the passive voice and the participial phrase and explain them.

Distinguish the simple present and present progressive

Give an example of a misuse of the future tense and explain it.

Explain modality in grammar

Explain Subject-verb Inversion

Distinguish while from during.

Distinguish before/ago and later/after

Distinguish in, within, and after

Distinguish because, because of, and due to.

Distinguish farther from further.

Distinguish little, less, and lesser.

Explain subjunctive: present unreal.

Explain subjunctive: past unreal.

Explain mixed subjunctive.

Explain subjunctive+SV inversion

Explain I wish, and as if subjunctive.

Phrase and Clause

Distinguish phrase and clause.

What is run-on sentence?

What are four cohesive devices necessary in connecting two sentences?

Conjunction and Relative Pronoun

Give examples of conjunctions and relative pronouns.

Colon and Semi-colon

Distinguish the use of colon and semi-colon.

How are colon and semi-colon similar?

Subject

Define subject.

Agent

Define agent.

Direct Object and Indirect Object

Distinguish direct object and indirect object.

Modifier/Modified

Distinguish modifier and modified.

Distinguish pre-modifier and post-modifier. Give an example of each.

Why should the modifier and the modified be placed next to each other?

Clarity

What two questions should the writer/speaker think about for clarity?

Conciseness

Explain conciseness. Give an example of a flowery sentence and improve it.

S.M.A.R.T.

Explain S.M.A.R.T.

ANSWERS

Sentence Completion Question Set 1

1. D	4. B	7. B
2. A	5. E	8. E
3. E	6. C	9. A

Sentence Completion Question Set 2

10. B	13. B	16. C
11. C	14. B	17. D
12. C	15. E	18. A

Reading Comprehension Question Set 1 -Narrative

1. A	4. C	7. D	10. C
2. C	5. B	8. E	
3. B	6. A	9. D	

Reading Comprehension Question Set 2 -Expository

1. C	4. B	7. C	10. E
2. D	5. C	8. B	11. E
3. B	6. D	9. D	

Reading Comprehension Question Set 3 -Narrative

10. C	12. A	14. A	16. B
11. B	13. E	15. B	17. C

Reading Comprehension Question Set 4 -Expository

12. D	15. B	18. C	21. A
13. C	16. A	19. E	
14. A	17. E	20. C	

REFERENCES

Miller, C. (1984). Genre as Social Action. *Quarterly Journal of Speech 70*. p. 151–167.

Pitkin, W. L., Jr. (1973). A Pedagogical Model of Discourse Structure. Unpublished doctoral dissertation, University of Southern California, Los Angeles

Schleppegrell, M. (2004). *The Language of Schooling: A Functional Linguistics Perspective*. Mahwah, New Jersey: Lawrence Erlbaum.

Made in the USA
Charleston, SC
12 June 2014